Shared Governance

Shared Governance

A More Meaningful Approach in Higher Education

Perry R. Rettig

ROWMAN & LITTLEFIELD
Lanham • Boulder • New York • London

Published by Rowman & Littlefield
An imprint of The Rowman & Littlefield Publishing Group, Inc.
4501 Forbes Boulevard, Suite 200, Lanham, Maryland 20706
www.rowman.com

6 Tinworth Street, London SE11 5AL, United Kingdom

British Library Cataloguing in Publication Information Available

Library of Congress Cataloging-in-Publication Data
Includes bibliographic references.

ISBN 978-1-4758-5473-2 (cloth : alk. paper)
ISBN 978-1-4758-5474-9 (pbk. : alk. paper)
ISBN 978-1-4758-5475-6 (Electronic)

∞ ™ The paper used in this publication meets the minimum requirements of American National Standard for Information Sciences—Permanence of Paper for Printed Library Materials, ANSI/NISO Z39.48-1992.

Shared Governance *is dedicated to my wife—Dr. Jeri-Mae G. Astolfi. Her exceptional and professional expertise as a piano performer and a professor gave me stamina and dedication to complete this endeavor. She was able to help me bring clarity to thought by challenging new ideas as we discussed evolving iterations of the manuscript. Similarly, I dedicate this book to all those leaders who came before us. We stand on your shoulders and endeavor to move forward. Finally, I dedicate this conceptual thinking to my peers in colleges and universities who persevere within their current organizational structures and who endeavor to do better. It is my sincere hope you will find the concepts in this book challenging and a place for you to begin your own collegial and democratic dialogue.*

Contents

List of Tables and Figure   ix

Preface   xi

Acknowledgments   xv

Introduction   xvii

1   Shared Governance Then and Now   1

2   Higher Education Organizational Suppositions   17

3   What If?   37

4   Here's How   63

5   Back to the Future   95

Bibliography   121

About the Author   129

List of Tables and Figure

TABLES

Table 4.1 Democratic (Political) Governance Model 64
Table 4.2 Corporate Governance Model 64
Table 4.3 K–12 School Governance Model 65
Table 4.4 Higher Education Shared Governance Model 66
Table 4.5 Pillar Responsibility Matrix 73
Table 5.1 Democratic Principles Matrix 105

FIGURE

Figure 5.1 K–12 School System Governance Pyramid 101

Preface

Today's system of shared governance was borne from a rather dystopian view of American organizational authority and politics. While both the political and business worlds have changed over the decades in this country, higher education governance has not kept pace. In fact, it has devolved into a lethargy incapable of making necessary change.

The best days of shared governance are behind us, at least in its present iteration. The heydays of the late 1960s through the early years of the 1990s provided faculty and administration great power and authority in running our institutions of higher learning. College presidents and their faculty held preeminent influence in decision making at their institutions.

Prior to these heady times for the internal constituents in colleges and universities the power structures favored external bodies, namely boards of trustees. Such bodies hired the executive and instructors to carry out their visions. Very slowly over time, executive structures began to take preeminence in higher education governance as the pendulum of power swung from parochial lay leaders to a professional class.

For decades American institutions of higher education have been governed by an antiquated model of shared governance. The model gained strength and a robust character in the 1800s through the first half of the twentieth century. A number of internal and external changes occurred across the landscape that, however, have eroded the shared nature of shared governance over the past fifty years and has only accelerated in the past two decades.

It is time to examine the presuppositions that have abraded our governance approaches and brought us to our current condition. "One of higher education's most distinctive values is its commitment to shared governance. Simply put, shared governance is a fundamental principle of inclusion in key areas of institutional responsibility and decision making."[1]

We have lost sight of these values and the roles we must collectively play in carrying out our governance responsibilities. "Because times have changed in the higher education sector, it is also important to ask whether and how the practice of shared governance has adapted and whether further change is necessary."[2]

Citing the work of Dr. Steven Bahls, the Association of Governing Boards (AGB) Board of Directors noted, "The current practice of shared governance works just fine when there aren't any problems. It breaks down as soon as the institution faces a significant challenge."[3] Further, Colleen Flaherty wrote, "While most presidents and board members from both public and private institutions believe that shared governance is working, they believe it could be more effective."[4]

Indeed, it is time for change in our shared governance structure and processes. As a matter of fact, quite often, failure to follow shared governance protocols lead to faculty votes of no confidence in their presidents.[5] But, why all these problems with shared governance?

Quite frankly, eminent higher education organizational leader Clark Kerr summed it up best: "The campus is inherently difficult to govern—even in theory."[6] MacTaggart expanded, "Sometimes what needs to be changed is not the institution or its operations, but its leadership structure and practices. The board role now requires greater fiscal oversight, better understanding of strategy and organizational capacity, and deeper engagement."[7] Mitchell and King went further:

> Colleges are confusing, bewildering, and complex places with storied traditions, antiquated governance practices, and competing constituencies. Even worse, however, is that many of the key leadership groups—especially trustees but including faculty and senior staff—are ill equipped to advise and govern a modern college or university. The end result is an erosion of good will among key stakeholders, often leading to institutional inertia, and in the extreme, debilitating chaos.[8]

Trustees and presidents are not the only groups to feel the frustration with current shared governance practices. Professor of Philosophy at Vanderbilt University, John Lachs, perhaps captures the sentiments of too many of his colleagues across the nation: "It takes years of rank and the bittersweet experience of extensive committee service to realize that faculty influence on the operation of the university is an illusion, and that shared governance is a myth." He added, "A cynical person may suppose that the charade is sustained in order to exhaust the faculty with meaningless tasks so they don't actually give trouble to management."[9]

Faculty have lost their collective voice, the organizations are too complex for a singular executive decider, and boards do not have sufficient expertise or background. These concerns indicate a need for a real, meaningful, and purposeful faculty role in shared governance. As a matter of fact, a renewed examination and rejuvenation of the entire shared governance model is crucial. "In a time of serious challenges to higher education . . . shared governance can be an essential institutional asset."[10]

Larry Gerber wrote of the primacy of faculty centrality in shared governance: "[F]aculty members, by virtue of their professional expertise in scholarship and teaching, ought to be centrally involved in college and university governance." He added, "From its inception, the AAUP recognized that academic freedom and faculty governance are, as a 1994 statement put it, so 'intricately linked' that one could not thrive without the other."[11] Yet, their role must be active, not merely pro forma.

The role of faculty in the concept of shared governance has been a primary focus of the American Association of University Professors (AAUP) since 1940. In fact, AAUP, American Council on Education (ACE), and AGB all collaborated to create the seminal 1966 Statement on Government of Colleges and Universities.[12] This collective statement remains today as the seminal document for contemporary shared governance thought.

This statement . . . calls for shared responsibility among the different components of institutional government and specifies areas of primary responsibility for governing boards, administrations, and faculties. It remains the association's central policy document relating to academic governance.

It has been supplemented over the years by a series of derivative policy statements, including those on faculty governance and academic freedom; budgetary and salary matters; financial exigency; the selection, evaluation, and retention of administrators; college athletics; governance and collective bargaining; and the faculty status of college and university librarians.[13]

So, a better model existed, but we have veered away over time. It was better but not sufficient; even it would be outdated, today. In this book, we will reexamine the initial model and look at other governance models that might make the original more contemporary. We will do this examination after considering founding democratic principles of our nation to see how they might impact our work. Indeed, it is the contention of this book that by using these seminal democratic principles and including staff and students in shared governance, the original intent of AAUP's 1966 Statement on Government of Colleges and Universities can be realized and improved upon.

NOTES

1. AGB, "AGB Board of Directors' Statement on Shared Governance." Washington, DC: Association of Governing Boards, (2017a): 1.

2. AGB, "Shared Governance: Changing with the Times." Washington, DC: Association of Governing Boards (2017b): 3.

3. Ibid. AGB, (2017a): 3.

4. Colleen Flaherty, "Surveys of Presidents and Board Members Suggests Shared Governance Matters to them but could be Improved Upon." Inside Higher Ed., (2016): 1.

5. Susan Whealler-Johnston, "Why Boards should Care about Shared Governance." *Trusteeship.* AGB. (September/October 2017): 2.

6. Clark Kerr, "Governance and Function." *Daedalus.* (99)1. The MIT Press, (Winter 1970): 108–121. www.jstor.org/stable/20023936.

7. Terrence MacTaggart, *Leading Change: How Boards and Presidents Build Exceptional Academic Institutions.* Washington, DC: AGB Press, (2011): 16.

8. Brian Mitchell and Joseph King. 2018. *How to Run a College: A Practical Guide for Trustees, Faculty, Administrators, and Policymakers* (Baltimore, MD: Johns Hopkins University Press, 2018), ix.

9. John Lachs, "Shared Governance is a Myth," *The Chronicle of Higher Education,* (February 6, 2011): 2.

10. AGB, "Shared Governance: Is OK Good Enough?" Washington, DC: AGB, (2016): 1.

11. Larry Gerber, "College and University Governance: How the AAUP has Established Widely Accepted Norms of Shared Governance," Washington, DC: American Association of University Professors (January/February 2015).www.aaup.org/article/college-and-university-governance.

12. American Association of University Professors, "1966 Statement on Government of Colleges and Universities." Washington, DC: www.aaup.org/report/statement-government-colleges-and-universities (1966).

13. AAUP, "Shared Governance." Washington, DC: American Association of University Professors (2017b). www.aaup.org/our-programs/shared-governance.

Acknowledgments

I will be forever indebted to several colleagues who helped me pull this project together with a sense of pragmatism. Katy Coker, Kim Crawford, and Kanler Cumbass each wrote reflective essays from their own perspectives in developing several of the concepts put forth in this book as they led the creation or renewal of staff and student governance. Likewise, Cat Wiles provided tremendous support in creating tables and formatting the manuscript into its present form.

Beyond my daily personal contacts with these individuals, I interacted with the knowledge and experiences of many other professionals and scholars. The collective wisdom of our predecessors can be found in the archives of AAUP, AGB, and ACE. The time spent visiting these websites, journals, and archives will be critical to any person serious in embarking on improving shared governance.

Further, in writing *Shared Governance*, I have benefitted immensely from reading the works of individual scholar/practitioners. I do need to make particular mention of these mentors of afar: Steven Bahls, William Bowen and Eugene Tobin, Patrick Dolan, Larry Gerber, Clark Kerr, Terrence Mac-Taggart, Gary Olson, and Robert Scott. Their insights and groundwork has enabled today's practitioners to make the conceptual a pragmatic reality.

Introduction

This book is about taking a critical eye to our extant governance structures in higher education, as they currently exist, looking at external contemporary organizational models and seminal democratic principles, and then reimagining a new model that will capitalize on the strengths of our constituent groups while at the same time maintaining those essential features of any democratic body—those that we hold to so dearly as a nation.

From this examination of these early ideals, we can examine the very nature of our presuppositions which characterize the changing model and thereby speculate upon new suppositions. Then, with this contemporary footing, a new model and understanding of shared governance can be envisioned that builds upon the original intent of shared governance along with those of a potentially more nimble and broadly defined model.

Woven throughout each chapter of this book is a story of Sam. Sam is the new vice president for enrollment management and marketing at Founders University. She came through the ranks of faculty, academic dean, and then vice president for academic affairs (VPAA) before landing her new position.

In her emerging story we find Sam struggling with the current circumstances of decision-making in a professional organization such as Founders, knowing that there must be a better way to lead. In collaboration with various constituents and colleagues, she attempts to create a new model, a new understanding, of shared governance. These altruistic attempts are met with a mix of both obfuscation and excitement.

Chapter 1, "Shared Governance Then and Now," sets the historical context of shared governance for colleges and universities in the United States. It begins at the beginning by describing how our nation's institutions of higher learning were governed at their inception. It continues by following the evolution of a need for a governing executive, followed by the development of a professional faculty. This led to a modern model of shared governance, but perhaps more robust than we have, today.

It will draw upon foundational understandings and seminal documents of shared governance in order to help us understand the purpose and original intent of the model. Each of the three pillars of shared governance will have their distinctive authorities delineated. Limitations of this model will then be noted and concluded by a detailed discussion of the contemporary "corporatization" of the higher education model.

Chapter 2, "Higher Education Organizational Suppositions," examines the philosophical underpinnings under which past and current models were created. It details the way things are today and why. This chapter enumerates the scientific/industrial, corporate, and cultural influences that created our contemporary model. This has led to the birth of bureaucracy and to the fields of organizational behavior and organizational theory. The focus will delve into the organizational theories that serve as the basis for our shared governance models, but it will also delineate the flaws of these views and the model itself.

Through the lens of critical theory, we will take a close examination of our presuppositions to how we organize and operate our colleges and universities. Through lessons learned from open systems theories we will better understand the nature of employees and the organizations in which they work. This will then serve as a hint of a bridge to democratic principles of shared governance.

Chapter 3, "What If?," examines postmodern, dynamic, and natural understandings of the human organization. This chapter then discusses the change process and how employees react to it. From that premise, we will visit how democratic structures and approaches support change. The first half of the chapter concludes with an analysis of concerns about such democratic structures and approaches.

The latter half of chapter 3 moves directly into a portrayal of our nation's founding democratic values and principles—those that relate most directly to the workplace. This analysis is done via a review of our founding documents: The Declaration of Independence, the United States Constitution and Amendments to the Constitution, and the Bill of Rights. This is followed with a description of how these political ideals should impact the workplace. The chapter concludes with an essay written by a college staff member describing her journey to create and implement a staff council.

Chapter 4, "Here's How," begins with an analysis of our nation's political governance model and the responsibilities of the three coequal branches of government. It then moves to a description of the modern corporate model of governance with its less than coequal anchors and their associated responsibilities. From this foundation, the chapter turns back to explore the shared governance model of contemporary higher education.

This chapter then shifts to a detailed portrayal of the responsibilities of each of the three pillars as originally designed along with a new examination of what could be—how some subtle changes or expectations might begin to change the relationships among these three pillars of shared governance. We conclude with an essay written by a former Student Government Association (SGA) president in which he discusses examples of what has and hasn't worked in his experience creating an active student voice in shared governance.

We conclude in chapter 5, "Back to the Future," by envisioning what might be a new contemporaneous conceptual model of shared governance. It will spend a great deal of focus on cultural understandings of shared leadership, principles, and processes that need to be in place for this new model to become a reality. It will require revisiting and reimagining governance roles, but most importantly, it will require a new conception of leadership, for everyone.

It will also feature a stronger and more pragmatic role of students in the governance process. After all, higher education's original purpose was to prepare a learned citizenry, and we should be the living laboratory for our future leaders. An essay from an associate dean of student engagement where she discusses the processes she used to help give students their voices in governance and leadership concludes this chapter.

Chapter 1

Shared Governance Then and Now

I enjoy talking to you. Your mind appeals to me. It resembles my own mind except that you happen to be insane.[1]

George Orwell, *1984*

The path of shared governance in our nation's institutions of higher education has been neither smooth nor straight. It has had many critics and has been prone to pressures from both within and from without. These pressures most often mirror those of the organizational culture of the country, yet not necessarily with great forethought or insight.

At the origination of America's colleges, little thought of faculty governance or rights existed. Higher education governance was left in the hands of lay leaders and clergy. In fact, it wasn't until the industrialization of the West and the professionalization of American research did faculty governance emerge.

These changes to the national culture forced changes at the institutional level. "The twin pillars of shared governance and academic freedom helped to support an environment that was both hospitable to scholars seeking to create new knowledge and intellectually challenging for the unprecedented numbers of students who began entering college after World War II."[2]

Larry Gerber explained that the industrializing nation demanded a more professional workforce:

In turn, colleges needed more highly trained research and career-oriented scholars. [I]ncreasingly professionalized faculty members demanded not only academic freedom in their research and teaching but also a larger degree of control over academic decision making as a matter of professional right and responsibility. Just as practitioners of the traditional professions of law and

1

medicine in the United States had begun in the nineteenth century more effectively to assert claims to greater autonomy and self-government on the basis of
their expertise. . . .[3]

Shared governance took the form we know today in the Age of Aquarius.
While it pales in the present compared to then, our understanding of the
rights of faculty came of age at this point of tumultuous cultural change.
"By the 1960s, the general principle of shared governance had become a
widely accepted norm in American higher education. . . . There was thus
a direct correlation between the development of a professionalized faculty,
an increasing faculty role in institutional governance, and the unparalleled
quality achieved by American higher education in the second half of the
twentieth century."[4]

In 1966, the American Association of University Professors (AAUP), the
American Council on Education (ACE), and the Association of Governing
Boards of Universities and Colleges (AGB) jointly issued the Statement
on Government of Colleges and Universities. "This statement attempted to
affirm the importance of shared governance and state some common principles."[5] Foremost was the principle of joint effort in managing these complex
organizations and the primacy of the role of faculty in curriculum, research,
faculty status, and student expectations.

With all this said, shared governance and the role of faculty reached its
zenith in the last half of the twentieth century, but the influence of faculty has
waned in the first two decades of the twenty-first century. What has caused
this drifting phenomenon?

We turn, again, to the insights of retired history professor of Auburn University, Larry Gerber. "The significant increase in the size of many American
institutions of higher education made possible the greater specialization of
faculty and also created a new organizational context in which issues of institutional governance were addressed."[6] Moreover:

> The increasing use of contingent faculty would become part of a larger trend
> toward the corporatization of American colleges and universities in which busi-
> ness models of management provided an alternative to the shared-governance
> approach that has risen to prominence in the 1960s. The significant growth in
> the number of two-year institutions, in which faculty generally enjoyed less
> prestige and professional status and hence were less likely to gain authority over
> academic decision making, also served to limit the practices of shared gover-
> nance in a rapidly expanding sector of American higher education.[7]

The professor in contemporary American higher education is highly
trained and specialized with an ever-increasing demand for scholarship.
The institutions in which they work have become enormously complex and

bureaucratic with high degrees of external accountability and internal administrative oversight.

There is a greater reliance on adjunct faculty to carry out the mission of these institutions, so there are now fewer professional career faculty able and willing to assert their roles and responsibilities of shared governance. The profession, with a little help from the outside, has done this to itself. Together, this has ultimately resulted in a deprofessionalization of the professoriate.

Rick Seltzer interviewed former president of Bucknell University and Washington & Jefferson College Brian C. Mitchell who stated, "Failing to professionalize governance isn't good for anyone. There should be a clear delineation of authority and a clear understanding—and a transparent understanding—of how power is executed on a college campus."[8]

These changes require a reconceptualization of shared governance. But, in order to reimagine a contemporaneous model, it is necessary to revisit the purpose of shared governance in higher education.

It is the contention of this book that reestablishing democratic norms and principles in the governance of our institutions of higher learning will again make shared governance meaningful. Eminent scholar Clark Kerr explained: "The university is also, to some degree, a democracy. Decisions are made that require the consent of the governed; rules are issued; and discipline is exercised."[9] Mitchell and King added, "The best way to manage a college or university—accounting for scale—is to put the 'sharing' back into shared governance."[10]

With an eye to current issues, the 2017 AGB Board of Directors' statement on shared governance noted, "In higher education's volatile environment, shared governance is essential. It adds substantial value to institutional progress and innovation. In fact, responsibility and accountability for addressing colleges' and universities' thorniest challenges often rest with multiple parties."[11]

By recapturing the responsibility of the mission, the constituents take ownership of their profession. "The rationale behind self-governance in higher education grows out of centuries-old tradition as well as the modern-day missions of colleges and universities. . . . Self-governance and self-regulation are crucial to institutional quality and integrity in American higher education."[12]

Therefore, the original purpose of shared governance was and continues to be the same: to provide for shared decision-making (and consequently shared responsibility) in the execution of the institution's mission and to protect the sovereignty of academic freedom. "Shared" does not necessarily mean "equal," however. This point will be explicated later in this book.

Conventional models of shared governance have established a tripartite, albeit unequal, structure. "The truth is that all legal authority in any university originates from one place and one place only: its governing board."[13] Olson goes on to stipulate that day-to-day operations are delegated to the president who further assigns additional responsibilities to other administration and staff. Faculty have distinct responsibilities and oversight to be explained later in this chapter.

Broadly speaking, boards of trustees are primarily responsible for making certain the college or university remains true to its mission, fiduciary oversight, strategic planning, and the evaluation of the president. The AGB further delineates specific duties of boards:

- Ensuring the integrity of the mission,
- Guarding academic quality, institutional autonomy, and academic freedom,
- Guarding fiscal integrity,
- Engaging effectively and appropriately with students, faculty, staff, alumni, and the community,
- Selecting, supporting, assessing, and compensating the president,
- Overseeing strategic planning, and
- Regularly assessing board performance, policies, and practices.[14]

As noted above, while boards of trustees hold ultimate authority and responsibility for their institutions, they delegate daily operational responsibilities to the president who in turn oversees faculty and staff in their work. Robert Scott cautions, "Ideally, boards should be partners with the campus president. Board members are expected to be experts in an area of concern to the institution without meddling in its affairs."[15]

The 1966 joint statement of AAUP, ACE, and AGB is universally accepted as the definitive statement of shared governance.[16] This document explicates the responsibilities of each arm of the tripartite governance body. Of equal import is the stress upon "joint effort" of all three in meeting the institution's mission. Numerous scholars cite this seminal document. Larry Gerber extrapolated that while each body has specified responsibilities and expertise, "joint effort" in all areas is critical.[17] Again, not all efforts are equal, however.

Bowen and Tobin refer to such efforts as "consultative rights." This is a model whereby "faculty would serve as co-managers, framing and implementing education policies and long-range planning affecting their institution's physical plant, budgeting, procedures affecting salary increases, and the appointment of the president and senior academic leaders."[18]

Robert Scott ties the relationship between the bodies together in exquisite fashion:

A university or college requires a form of covenant between the faculty and the president, just as there needs to be one between the board and the president. The covenant is based on a trust that there will be no surprises and that there will be appropriate and adequate consultation on major issues. Consultation does not mean obedience, but it does mean taking seriously the suggestions and objections of the faculty.[19]

In an interesting description of faculty and president roles, AGB explains the overarching role of boards. "It is up to the faculty and administration to uphold and improve academic quality. But it is up to the board to understand it and to see that it gets done."[20]

With adroit clarity, Susan Whealler Johnston explains, "Typically, presidents are charged with institutional leadership, vision, strategic planning, and daily management, while faculty are charged with educational design and delivery. In shared governance, faculty have authority and responsibility for all things related to *who* teaches *what* to *whom* [emphasis in original]—who the faculty are, what the curriculum is, and who the admitted students are."[21]

The AAUP Statement on Government of Colleges and Universities describes the essential roles of faculty:

> The faculty has primary responsibility for such fundamental areas as curriculum, subject matter and methods of instruction, research, faculty status, and those aspects of student life which relate to the educational process. . . . The faculty sets the requirements for the degrees offered in course, determines when the requirements have been met, and authorizes the president and board to grant the degrees thus achieved. Faculty status and related matters are primarily a faculty responsibility; this are includes appointments, reappointments, decisions not to reappoint, promotions, the granting of tenure, and dismissal. . . . The faculty should actively participate in the determination of policies and procedures governing salary increases.[22]

The AGB further defined the responsibilities of faculty, as well as both the chief executive officer and the board of trustees.

Responsibilities of Faculty:
- Ensure academic quality,
- Curriculum and instruction development and oversight,
- Set and oversee admissions standards,
- Research,
- Oversight of faculty status, and
- Operate with ethical standards.

Responsibilities of Presidents:
- Provide institutional leadership,
- Create and sustain institution vision,
- Ensure academic quality and autonomy,
- Lead strategic planning,

- Oversee day-to-day operations,
- Communicate with various internal and external constituencies,
- Fundraising and advancement, and
- Operate with ethical standards.

Responsibilities of Boards of Trustees:
- Fiduciary oversight,
- Ensure principles for shared governance are followed,
- Hiring, evaluating, and supporting the president,
- Ensure the institution is beholden to its mission,
- Strategic planning,
- Ensure all institutional policies are current and implemented,
- Protect academic freedom and institutional autonomy, and
- Operate with ethical standards.[23]

Faculty are represented in the model of shared governance via a representative body—the faculty senate. Senates serve three distinct purposes: to share and consult in institutional decision-making; to represent concerns of faculty to administration and to the board of trustees; and to police themselves with respect to the hiring, the evaluation, the promotion and granting of tenure, and the dismissal of fellow faculty colleagues.[24] With respect to the latter, such internal policing is parallel to that of the medical and legal professions.

Mitchell and King noted, "They must rise above internal politics, 'trust but verify' the policy and program direction proposed, be open to change, and educate and advocate for faculty interests."[25] Bowen and Tobin added, "It can be helpful to have an established structure in place that gives individuals a 'place to go' to express displeasure on matters of any kind . . . [f]aculty senates . . . exist to meet this need."[26]

A final yet equally critical role of faculty senates is that of moving the institution's agenda forward. Clara Chan interviewed former Northwestern University faculty senate president Stephen F. Eisenman who said, "An active, engaged faculty senate is crucial for a university to be progressive and dynamic and innovative. You want a university where new ideas are generated from the ground up, not the top down."[27] Terrence MacTaggart extended these thoughts:

> Involving these intelligent, well-educated thinkers early in the change process has several advantages. On a pragmatic level, professors are more apt to buy into changes that they have a hand in making. If faculty representatives are persuaded that change is inevitable and that change they help to engineer is preferable to that imposed upon them, they will help sell the new order to their colleagues. Bringing faculty to the table early also adds thoughtful scrutiny to the change process and results in better ideas overall.[28]

The board of trustees, the president (and administration), and the faculty (through faculty senate and representative committees) each hold specific roles and responsibilities in the shared governance of their institutions. The best run colleges and universities have governance systems that provide a great deal of respect and autonomy for one another, enjoy high degrees of transparency, and most often find overlap in their work and communications with one another.

With that said, shared governance has limitations and various concerns for each of these distinct bodies. Governing boards may not provide sufficient oversight or guidance, presidents and their administration may work too unilaterally or without adequate transparency, and faculty senates may grind decision-making to a halt or obfuscate in times of change.

In the introductory sentence of its 2017 White Paper, AGB reported, "Shared governance is one of the basic tenets of higher education, and yet there is considerable evidence that it is not generally well understood by its primary participants—faculty members, presidents, and members of boards of trustees."[29] Even more concerning, Flaherty warned, "[V]ery few presidents or board members see shared governance as sharing 'equal rights' with other constituencies, including faculty members."[30]

Aside from a general lack of appreciation for the purpose and the principles of shared governance, what are the specific issues at the board and executive levels? Three primary concerns most often cited are: the model for decision-making is too slow,[31] the nature of the higher education enterprise is too complex,[32] and the board sizes are too large. To the last point, Clark Kerr stated, "Massive size is an enemy of effective governance in the academic world."[33]

Clearly, however, critics of contemporary governance structures point to the biggest concern as the corporatization of today's boards. As fiscal solvency is the driving imperative for keeping our institutions of higher learning operating, boards of trustees have shifted to corporate models and corporate executives to run those corporate models.[34]

Kezar and Holcombe warn, "The current push for greater top-down leadership is counterproductive to today's higher education landscape and is in misalignment with research on effective organizations that demonstrates the need for shared leadership."[35] Mitchell and King, on the other hand, clarify: "But in the end, colleges and universities are businesses. They operate by different rules, however, than corporate America—an essential difference that must be understood if shared governance is to work."[36]

This corporatization of boards has, in turn, led to the corporatization of the executive or presidency.[37] With that stipulated, two pillars of shared governance—the board of trustees and the executive—have become de facto corporate in power and authority. This in turn has led to a diminished and inequitable role for the third pillar—the faculty.

Bjorn Stensaker and Agnete Vabo have used the term "managerialism" to describe this trend toward removing faculty from shared partnership in organizational decision-making.[38] Ami Zusman used the phrase "managed professionals" to describe this more recent phenomenon[39] (Zusman, 2005, 147).

Even more insidious is the notion that shared governance has become fake or a show. Through the lens of Critical Thoery, Kezar and Holcombe stated, "Shared leadership was primarily a rhetorical strategy used by vertical leaders to give the impression of inclusion and collaboration."[40]

Nearly all these issues could be resolved with induction and ongoing orientation for shared governance constituents, but most notably board members. "Some college and university board members know little more about higher education than what they remember from their days as students, what their children may have experienced, what they may have garnered when being asked for donations, or what they read or hear in news media."[41] As a remedy, the AGB has devoted an entire document *Effective Governing Boards* to describe in erudite fashion quality training for boards of trustees.[42]

This perception of lack of legitimate power has added to other concerns of faculty. Today's professors have increased pressures and demands on their time for research, academic advising, and in being held accountable for their student learning outcomes. Compounding this issue of lack of time[43] is the fact that the percentage of full-time tenured and tenure-track professors is declining in relation to adjunct instructors.[44]

Those supporting a more corporate model of higher education governance have their rationale. Gerber explained, "These critics consider the system of significant faculty autonomy and substantial responsibility for educational matters a form of governance that prevents necessary changes and frustrates efforts to bring greater accountability to American higher education."[45]

In a concurring finding from its 2017 survey, AGB explained, "Board members and presidents in particular lamented the length of time to make important decisions in the most common approaches to shared governance. They expressed concern that the current practice of shared governance impedes an institution's ability to be agile, flexible, and responsive in a rapidly changing environment—whether the issue was taking advantage of opportunities or responding to acute challenges."[46]

Further, Lachs reported, "Faculty members have no special competence in running organizations; many of them lack the practical sense required for making savvy and timely decisions concerning the complexities of institutional life. Moreover, they have little or no interest in the details of administration."[47]

While Scott asserted the critical importance of faculty representation in planning and decision-making, he noted that few want to participate in making budget cuts.[48] Bowen and Tobin, while advocating for the essential faculty voice in curricular development, warn that faculty should not be given the authority to veto such issues as program discontinuation.[49]

This chapter has provided a brief historical outline of shared governance in higher education before turning to describe the current state of decision-making in our institutions of higher learning. It concluded with a description of concerns of each of the three pillars (boards of trustees, chief executive officers, and faculty). Chapter 2 will describe the historical and cultural developments in the United States that brought about these changes as well as our current status. But for a moment, we turn our attention to our book's protagonist—Sam Sabbon.

SAM—TO MOLD A NEW REALITY

She recalled the lyrics of RUSH: "And the men who hold high places must be the ones who start to mold a new reality, one closer to the heart."[50] Sam knew she was destined to be a leader, and she vowed to make a difference when she was in a position of power. Her father named her Samantha but always called her Sam. He told her he named her for Uncle Sam, because she would make a difference in this world. As a matter of fact, the name Uncle Sam came from: United States of America. Sam always took great pride in her name.

Fast forward three meandering decades, and she had to pause as she looked out on the picturesque grounds of Founders University academic quad. After serving four years as VPAA, Sam now began her job as vice president for enrollment management over the summer but had grown disenchanted with her faculty senate. Over time its function devolved; it now held only static meetings with the occasional proclamation. Pro forma standing committees rarely met and had very little to report. But, Sam knew that these senate members were good professors. They cared about their students and the university, they were strong scholars, and they were deeply connected to their fields. For some reason, though, there was a sense of isolation and powerlessness.

There was so much potential that was just being wasted. Morale was low, faculty felt administration didn't value them, and this was the first institution that Sam worked at where there was no staff council. Where faculty felt underappreciated, staff members felt like second-class citizens. Sam knew that this was for good reason—they actually were treated that way.

That was it! Sam was going to make some changes around here; she was going to create a reform agenda. Sam was going to reinvigorate the faculty senate, and she was going to create a staff council. Step one was going to be a lunch with the faculty senate vice president—Sam felt the senate president was recalcitrant and would be a stick in the mud. Step two was going to be an appointment with the registrar (Beatriz)—an especially professional and

forward-thinking staff member, and Camille—the administrative assistant to
the vice president for enrollment management and marketing. Camille was
perhaps the strongest informal leader at Founders. She knew the school's history and everyone on campus. And, everyone on campus seemed to acquiesce
to her.

Beatriz and Sam had already started on their coffee drinks at the student commons when Camille came rushing in. She had texted that she was running a
few minutes late as she was "advising" a student. The women had ordered a
frappacino for Camille so they could jump right into the conversation.

"Why the secret meeting, Sam?" started Beatriz.

"Oh, I'm sorry if this seems secret or cryptic, Beatriz," came Sam's reply.
"I just don't want to get people stirred up or make any promises before we
even talk." While Sam wasn't whispering, she did speak in rather hushed
tones as the commons was filled with students, most of whom were still wak-
ing up. The coffee shop was always the most popular place at this time of
the morning.

Camille made come hither motions with her hand. "Well, go ahead. You
have us on the edge of our seats."

"I respect you both so much. You're highly regarded campus leaders, and
you can get things done."

Beatriz smiled, "Flattery will get you everywhere."

Sam continued, "This is the first university I have been at that does not
have a staff council or governing body for professional staff. I can't believe
it. Yet, we have such tremendous human assets, here. I want to start a staff
council!"

Camille and Beatriz looked at each other. Camille finally broke the silence
as she swirled her drink with a spoon. "Oh, I was hoping for some fun news."

The smile fell from Sam's face. "What do you mean?" she asked incredu-
lously. "This could be so exciting, and it's so important!" Sam lost all signs
of her hushed tones by now.

Camille paused a moment and lifted her finger as if to say, "I have a prescient point that I'm about to make." Then, she started. "Do we even have
administrative support? Things are fine the way they are. Why add extra work
for people and give people false hopes of power?" She looked back at her
frappacino.

"My goodness, Camille, of all people I hadn't expected you to feel this
way," replied Sam. She rubbed her chin and cast her eyes downward.

"Well, I'm sorry, Sam. It's just that people took these jobs as is. They
haven't had any desires to have authority. They work hard every day and
make a difference in the lives of our students. Wouldn't a staff council be

a lot more work? And, what purpose would it serve? Would we vote on things?"

Beatriz interjected. "Wait a moment, Camille. I'd like to hear more from Sam. I think this sounds intriguing. I want our colleagues to feel empowered."

Sam quickly smiled. "I don't want them to feel empowered; I want them to be empowered." She went on. "I know our staff feel like second-class citizens. They feel faculty and administration don't listen. I want to give them voice. By formally sanctioning them, we can only be better as an organization. Besides, I think it's the right way to treat people."

"Thanks, Sam," came Beatriz's response. "I do share some of Camille's reluctance. We've all served on committees, though, where we end up being the note-takers, and when we make comments it's as if no one cares what we say. Then, when a committee finally makes a decision it gets overturned by the administration."

Camille nodded her head. "In fact, that's the main reason staff beg off of committee involvement, Sam."

"I do hear you guys," Sam mumbled. "I've certainly had more than my share of committee frustrations. I think a big part of the problem is that when committees are formed they are never told what is expected of them. In other words, do they make recommendations or do they make decisions? My experience is that people don't like to have their decisions overturned. But, if they know they are simply to make recommendations to their bosses, then they can more easily live with it."

"Well said, Sam," Camille followed.

"In any case, today's conversation is more rhetorical—just to get us to start thinking. Let's just finish our coffee and plan to get together again next week," Sam smiled slightly.

Sam had added an item to the president's cabinet agenda. It simply read, "Staff Council." Around the conference room table sat President Lloyd Davis; vice president of administration and finance, Henry Hutchins; vice president for advancement, Peter Gabrielse; vice president for student affairs, enrollment management, and athletics, Dirk Zentkowski; and chief information officer, Fareed Musa; and of course, Samantha Sabbon. Joining the group today was also special assistant to the president, Dr. Meng Xiong.

The meeting started off with the obligatory round-robin of cabinet members going around the room giving updated reports. Sam felt much of this could be handled via email. In any case, the agenda did have a place for Old Business and for New Business. Under Old Business, VP Hutchins provided a handout showing the post-fall budget now that enrollments were certain. Enrollments were stable, but healthcare costs exceeded expectations. Possible

across-the-board budget cuts may be warranted. More discussion was to follow at the next cabinet meeting.

The mood in the meeting became a little more somber after that discussion. Meng Xiong then reminded the group that HEMetrics strategic planning
firm would arrive on campus next week to begin listening sessions for the
next five-year plan. Everyone nodded their heads in approval but their faces
betrayed only stoicism. Each of these seasoned veterans had gone through
previous strategic planning campaigns before. Some were internally driven,
but it was getting to be more and more the case that outside firms ran the
process with more and more complex data gathering and analysis. Already
heavy workloads would only be getting heavier.

President Davis then turned to Sam and waved his hand, palm up, as if to
say, "The table is yours." But he squinted with an air of caution.

Sam looked around the room. All eyes were upon her. She enjoyed meeting
in this stately presidential conference room. The legacy of decades' worth of
decisions had been made here, and she was now part of that unfolding history.
"Thank you, Lloyd. A few of us have broached the subject of starting a Staff
Council at Founders. We, of course, would start out small and formalize the
role, authority, and parameters of such a governance group. I am asking for
your assent and guidance," Sam stated glancing around the table.

With a furrowed brow, Dr. Davis interjected, "A number of you have
started this discussion already?" His hands, which had been folded, were
now gripping a pen as he jotted down a couple of words on his agenda. Sam
couldn't make out what he had written.

Samantha was startled for a moment. "I only chatted with two staff members about the idea over coffee."

"What would be the purpose of such a council?" questioned Peter Gabrielse. "You mentioned a new governance group. I mean, why would we want
to give formal authority to yet another group of people on campus. It would
seem to me that this would make our jobs more difficult and slow down the
decision-making process. The faculty senate is already difficult enough to
work with. Besides, we had a Staff Committee twenty years ago, and it fell
apart. They put together social events and attendance dwindled. Everyone felt
it was a waste of time, and I think morale suffered because of it."

Sam felt defensive, "They have so much to offer us, and this would help
staff morale, because it wouldn't be about planning social events." She knew
her ears were red, and she didn't like being judged as the only woman in the
room.

The back-and-forth of comments, questions, and concerns stumbled along
for a few minutes, but it seemed like an eternity to Sam. Finally, President
Davis subtly waved his hand over the agenda. "Sam, while there may be some
skepticism around this table, I am more than a bit intrigued by your idea.

Please flesh it out a bit more, and we can discuss it when you're ready." He nodded in approval, and adjourned the meeting.

Sam had hoped for a more enthusiastic response from her colleagues, but at least there was a possibility. But, how was she going to "flesh out this idea?" In any case, she now turned her attention to the faculty senate.

Sam and faculty senate vice president Patrick McQuinlan sat across from each other at a small outdoor table at Café LaMode across the street from campus. This was the second time they had lunch together. When Sam wrote to Patrick asking to get together for lunch she did so with excitement. Café LaMode was always bustling with activity. Sam liked it, because it was a good mix of college and community folks. Now, she was a bit reluctant. But, here they were.

After placing their orders and sitting at a small table for two, Sam began. "Patrick, I want you to keep an open mind."

Patrick seemed a bit taken aback. He pulled his head back and tilted it slightly to the right. "You don't think I am fair-minded, Sam?"

"No, no, no, Patrick. I'm sorry. I've just have had enough skepticism lately."

Patrick smiled, "Go on, Samantha."

"Well, to be honest, Patrick," Sam continued, "I am just a bit disappointed in the Senate. They are such a great group of people, but we just don't seem to get anything of importance accomplished. I mean, what is our agenda for the year? What do we want to accomplish? It just seems like we're going through the motions. We have standing committees that don't even meet!"

"I'm with you, Sam. I am thinking of not running for another term after this one runs out. It seems like a waste of a few hours each month. I've got teaching, research, and real service to do. But, what are you thinking of?"

"I don't really know how to put it, Patrick. But, let's get these standing committees active. They each need to review their charge and actually meet. They then need to report to the full Senate. And, the Senate needs to have a couple of goals for the year."

Sam was about to answer, but they were interrupted by their server—Earnest. He placed a Greek BLT in front of Sam. However, the bacon was actually lamb. In front of Patrick, Earnest placed a beautiful plate of ratatouille. He also poured a bit more olive oil next to their bread bowl.

Patrick asked, "What kinds of goals do you have in mind, Sam?"

"I don't know. They don't need to be my goals. But, it would seem that the committees would have goals after they review their charges. Soon, we will be starting our strategic planning. It sure would be nice if the Senate had a couple of goals to take into the planning. Oh, and I have another. I hear faculty continually complain about the quality of online/hybrid instruction. Why don't they own that concern and make a difference. Curriculum and instruction are under the purview of faculty, so I think the Faculty Senate should take the lead."

Now Patrick was grinning from ear-to-ear. "Excellent. Your enthusiasm, Sam, has got me going. Let's bring this up at our next Senate Executive Committee. The two of us can take the lead as partners. We may face some resistance, but how can they truly argue against us. We want to make the Senate meaningful!"

The two colleagues began to banter back-and-forth about ideas they had. They were interrupted when two students came to their table and started a social conversation with Patrick. Sam felt in a better frame of mind than when she arrived. She picked up the tab and left with a renewed sense of purpose. She didn't know what was ahead.

NOTES

1. George Orwell, *1984* (London, England: Secker and Warburg, 1949. Reprinted in 2003. Boston: Houghton Mifflin Harcourt), 334.

2. Larry Gerber, *The Rise and Decline of Faculty Governance: Professionalization and the Modern American University* (Baltimore, MD: Johns Hopkins University Press, 2014), 2. For a thoughtful and erudite historical narrative of the history of shared governance in the United States, the reader will not find a better book than Gerber's.

3. Gerber, *The Rise and Decline of Faculty Governance*, 4.

4. Ibid., 6.

5. Gary Olson, "Exactly What is 'Shared Governance?'" *The Chronicle of Higher Education* (July 23, 2009), 1.

6. Gerber, *The Rise and Decline of Faculty Governance*, 29.

7. Ibid., 83. Gerber further stipulated that governing board members and administrators have treated colleges as industries which has led to a deprofessionalization of the faculty and by reducing the number of full-time tenured faculty with part-time instructors (146–147). But even more importantly:

> The increasing use of part-time and non-tenure track faculty has undermined the practice of shared governance in several ways. The development of shared governance in the twentieth century was premised on the emergence of a professionalized faculty with the expertise required to make informal academic judgments and with a career-long commitment to advancing academic values that served the public interest. Most faculty members on contingent appointments, however, have little prospect of developing full-time careers at a college or university, and they are typically appointed without an expectation that they will engage in the full panoply of professional activities. . . . participation in institutional governance, [is] not usually part of their job descriptions. (147)

8. Rick Setlzer, "New Books Examine College Governance and How it can Adapt to Changing Times," *Inside Higher Education* (March 1, 2018), 1.

9. Clark Kerr, "Governance and Functions," *Daedalus* 99 (1) (Winter 1970), 108–121, 115, www.jstor.org/stable/20023936. Kerr expanded: "A missing link in governance in the United States is an over-all council of the total campus community—students, faculty, administrators, trustees, alumni. . . . Such a council would seek to evolve and preserve a consensus about the community as a whole and to protect the academic faith." 118.

10. Brian Mitchell and Joseph King, *How to Run a College: A Practical Guide for Trustees, Faculty, Administrators, and Policymakers* (Baltimore, MD: Johns Hopkins University Press, 2018), 15–16.

11. AGB, "AGB Board of Directors' Statement on Shared Governance" (Washington, DC: AGB, 2017a), 2.

12. AGB, "Effective Governing Boards: A Guide for Members of Governing Boards of Independent Colleges and Universities" (Washington, DC, 2014), 18.

13. Olson, "Exactly What is 'Shared Governance?'" 1.

14. Robert Scott, *How University Boards Work: A Guide for Trustees, Officers, and Leaders in Higher Education* (Baltimore, MD: Johns Hopkins University Press, 2018), 39.

15. Scott, *How University Boards Work*, 35.

16. AAUP, "Statement on Government of Colleges and Universities" (Washington, DC, 1966), aaup.org/report/statement-government-colleges-and-universities.

17. Gerber, *The Rise and Decline of Faculty Governance*, 97–98.

18. William Bowen and Eugene Tobin, *Locus of Authority: The Evolution of Faculty Roles in the Governance of Higher Education* (Princeton, NJ: Princeton University Press, 2015), 86–88.

19. Scott, *How University Boards Work*, 60.

20. AGB, "Effective Governing Boards,"16.

21. Susan Whealler Johnston, "Why Boards Should Care about Shared Governance," *Trusteeship* (Washington, DC: Association of Governing Boards of Universities and Colleges, September/October 2017), 2.

22. AAUP, "Statement on Government of Colleges and Universities" (Washington, DC: American Association of University Professors, 2017c), 4, www.aaup.org/report/statement-government-colleges-and-universities.

23. AGB, "Effective Governing Boards," 5–25. In this document, the association details in erudite fashion these particular responsibilities associated with boards of trustees, among others.

24. Larry Gerber, "College and University Governance: How the AAUP has Established Widely Accepted Norms of Shared Governance" (Washington, DC: American Association of University Professors, January–February 2015), 1, www.aaup.org/article/college-and-university-governance.

25. Mitchell and King, *How to Run a College*, 16.

26. Bowen and Tobin, *Locus of Authority*, 147.

27. Clara Chan, "A Common Plea of Professors: Why Can't My Faculty Senate Pull More Weight?" *The Chronicle of Higher Education* (July 6, 2017), 1.

28. Terrence MacTaggart, *Leading Change: How Boards and Presidents Build Exceptional Academic Institutions* (Washington, DC: AGB Press 2011), 35.

29. AGB, "AGB Board of Directors' Statement on Shared Governance," 1.

30. Colleen Flaherty, "Survey of Presidents and Board Members Suggests Shared Governance Matters to them But Could be Improved Upon," *Inside Higher Ed* (2016), 1, https://www.insidehighered.com/news/2016/09/29/survey-presidents-and-board-members-suggests-shared-governance-matters-them-could-be?width=77 5&height=500&iframe=true.

31. Bjorn Stensaker and Agnete Vabo, "Re-inventing Shared Governance: Implications for Organisational Culture and Institutional Leadership," *Higher Education Quarterly* 67 (3) (July 2013), 256.

32. AGB, "AGB Board of Directors' Statement on Shared Governance," 5.

33. Kerr, "Governance and Functions," 120.

34. Gerber, *The Rise and Decline of Faculty Governance*, 146.

35. Adrianna Kezar and Elizabeth Holcombe, "Shared Leadership in Higher Education: Important Lessons from Research and Practice" (Washington, DC: American Council on Education, 2017), 29: 2.

36. Mitchell and King, *How to Run a College*, 17.

37. Kerr, "Governance and Functions," 110.

38. Stensaker and Vabo, "Re-inventing Shared Governance," 2.

39. Ami Zusman, "Challenges Facing Higher Education in the Twenty-First Century," In Philip Altbach and Patricia Gumport, eds, *American Higher Education in the Twenty-First Century: Social, Political, and Economic Challenges* (Baltimore, MD: Johns Hopkins University Press, 2005), 147.

40. Kezar and Holcombe, "Shared Leadership in Higher Education," 18.

41. Scott, *How University Boards Work*, 13.

42. AGB, "Effective Governing Boards," 2014.

43. Gerber, *The Rise and Decline of Faculty Governance*, 8.

44. Flaherty, "Survey of Presidents and Board Members Suggests Shared Governance Matters to them But Could be Improved Upon," 3.

45. Gerber, *The Rise and Decline of Faculty Governance*, 20.

46. AGB, "AGB Board of Directors' Statement on Shared Governance," 9.

47. Larry Lachs, "Shared Governance is a Myth," *The Chronicle of Higher Education* (February 6, 2011), 2. Lachs went on to stipulate, "If education is primarily a business, managers hire the faculty. If universities are communities of students and scholars, faculty hire the managers. The difference between the two strategies is immense, because it determines the locus of power. Looked at from this perspective, it is even clearer that in today's universities, faculty members are employees with no say in the operation of their institutions," 2.

48. Scott, *How University Boards Work*, 57.

49. Bowen and Tobin, *Locus of Authority*, 168.

50. RUSH, "Closer to the Heart," *A Farewell to Kings*. Mercury Records, 1977.

Chapter 2

Higher Education Organizational Suppositions

The heretical mailed fist of American reality rises to the surface in the velvet glove of our every institutionalized endeavor.[1]

Eldridge Cleaver

When our country was primarily an agrarian nation, our institutions of higher learning were small and run by lay leaders. As the United States evolved into the Industrial Age, colleges and universities became much larger and complex. Since that era, however, the management and organizational structure of these American institutions have seen very little substantive change.[2]

The Scientific Revolution and the Industrial Age had tremendous implications for the management of not only the nation's manufacturing sector but for the management of our institutions of higher learning, as well. As our colleges and universities became larger and more complex and faculty became more highly credentialed and trained, they lost—and to a degree abdicated—some of their autonomy and power. The era of bureaucracy was born.

How did this happen? A confluence of two major events brought these changes about. First, the classical Newtonian sciences gained preeminence. Second, the Industrial Age became dominant. Together, they created the science of organizational administration which changed the power dynamics both in the corporate world and at our college campuses.

It is quite apparent that classical physics is founded on linear, mechanistic thinking. The foundation of this science is a study of the parts in a reductionistic way of looking at *things*. The notion of *things* is of critical importance to classical physics. This physics has the aim of reducing the whole into ever smaller parts. The classical sciences provided the framework for the scientific study of organizations; Frederick Taylor provided the scholarship.

17

An American with an engineering background, Taylor believed that organizations could be studied and rationally understood. His time and motion studies were conducted in order to organize each type of work so that time and effort were minimized and productivity was maximized. Basic features of this model are well known to all who have studied management. In order to provide for routine performance, there must be a standardization of tasks. Through a division of labor there is a specialization of tasks. While there is a *specialization* of tasks, the tasks become *standardized* within their specialization.

An impersonal hierarchy is necessary and is established through a pyramid model where the optimal number of people under any one person's span of control should be five to ten workers. This impersonal orientation is designed to treat all employees alike and to keep decisions objective and rational. There must also be a uniqueness of function where each department does its own work, and there should not be any duplication of work by other departments.

Finally, the formal connections within the organization are indicated on an organizational blueprint or flowchart of hierarchy and corresponding job responsibilities. This scientific movement to the understanding of organizations has had a profound influence on the structuring and management of these systems. Taylor conceptualized four principles of scientific management—two of which are pertinent for the discussion at hand:

• Establish a clear division of responsibility between management and workers, with management doing the goal-setting, planning and supervising, and workers executing the required tasks and
• Establish the discipline whereby management sets the objectives and the workers cooperate in achieving them.[3]

These principles of scientific management played a central role in the design of administration in this new era.

Large organizations were a byproduct of the Industrial Age. The industrial leaders needed ways to understand and manage these gigantic monolithic structures. The machines that were created in these factories served as a model for the organization of their own industries. Closed systems thinking was born, and the machine metaphor served as its exemplar. Industrialists thought that they could run their manufacturing systems like the machines they made, and in fact, they did manage their organizations in a corresponding fashion.

Closed systems thinking is all about efficiency and effectiveness. The goal is to maximize productivity. It is a positivistic or deterministic approach that requires linear, rational decision-making. French industrialist Henri Fayol had executive-level work experience, and he began the actual study of classical organizational thought. "He advocated that all managers perform five basic functions: planning, organizing, commanding, coordinating, and controlling."[4]

Still, Fayol advocated that administrators use these principles flexibly and that they use judgment in carrying out their responsibilities. This lesson seems to have been overlooked by many of our contemporary executives. According to notable systems thinker Peter Block, "We govern our organizations by valuing, above all else, consistency, control, and predictability."[5]

Max Weber—a German sociologist—concerned about arbitrary power in the hands of the few, formulated bureaucratic structures in order to legitimize authority in the hands of the experts.[6] Structurally, Weber believed that all good organizations should share certain characteristics for the purpose of efficiency.

While Weber advocated bureaucratic structures, he was also concerned that bureaucracies could become too strong or overbearing, and therefore, dangerous. This seems to be yet another lesson lost on many of our contemporary leaders. But as organizations got bigger, there grew a demand for greater differentiation, academic specialization, and bureaucratization.[7]

Critics of the Weberian model have always existed. They point out that such bureaucratization hurts staff morale and causes worker boredom. These same critics claim that communication patterns are not more efficient,[8] that workers have no control of their goals and work environment, and that there is a conflict between achievement and seniority. Charles Heckscher argued, "All of Weber's forms of legitimate authority are essentially structures of domination—that is, contexts in which the higher level can command *without giving a justification* [emphasis in original]."[9]

Bureaucratic practices also produce legalism—where frustrated workers follow their job descriptions to the letter, not working to their full potential. Feminists feel that these organizations are gender-biased. And, most interestingly, the Weberian model assumes that the subordinates have less technical expertise than their superiors.[10]

Again, the Weberian model assumes that the subordinates have less technical expertise than their superiors. This last point is crucial to our understanding of today's higher education culture. This hidden assumption is that our faculty and professional staff know less than the executive administrators.

Such assumptions are perilous. Mihaly Csikszentmihalyi warned, "The evidence suggests that the Industrial Revolution not only shortened the life spans of members of several generations, but made them more nasty and brutish as well."[11] Again, Max Weber proposed bureaucratic structures in order to make organizations more efficient, the work of the workers less ambiguous, and to take the power out of the hands of the few. The unintended result was the deprofessionalization of the organization—a loss of professional autonomy and decision-making.

But according to Francis X. Neumann Jr., "The Weberian bureaucracy was totally suitable to a Weberian world, for a world of industrial or second wave society, but it may not be altogether appropriate for the new and more complex environments [of today]."[12] This same notion would hold true for professional organizations.

These concerns have led practitioners and scholars alike to consider that classical organizations are, in fact, not very efficient. Management began to believe that in order to make workers more efficient, they needed to make the work environment more collegial. In other words, "A happy worker is a productive worker." This led to the birth of a new model—the Human Relations Approach.

Like all closed systems theories, the Human Relations Approach still had the primary aim of efficiency in organizations. This approach is also considered closed systems thinking because management still controls and manipulates the system, albeit, in a friendlier, gentler manner.

Mary Parker Follett was not a strict adherent to classical organizational thought. As a sociologist, she saw the importance of administrators working *with* their employees as opposed to dictating to them. Likewise, she believed that decisions should be contingent upon the context of the situation—a precursor to contingency theory.

Parker advocated that decisions be made by those closest to where the decisions would be impacted. And both vertical and horizontal communication paths need to be utilized across and up through the organization. The third principle requires departments and units to be able to coordinate, in a flexible manner, their efforts in order to meet the organization's demands. The fourth principle "recognizes that management is an ever-changing, dynamic process in response to emerging situations—a sharp contrast to traditional, static, classical views that sought to codify universal principles of action."[13]

The now famous Hawthorne studies helped shape the Human Relations movement. From these experiments, the social side of work dynamics proved to be certainly as important as the technical side. According to Owens:

New concepts were now available to the administrator to use in practice. Among them were (1) morale, (2) group dynamics, (3) democratic supervision, (4) personnel relations, and (5) behavioral concepts of motivation. The human relations movement emphasized human and interpersonal factors in administering the affairs of organizations. Supervisors, in particular, drew heavily on human relations concepts, stressing such notions as "democratic" procedures, "involvement," motivational techniques, and the sociometry of leadership.[14]

Therefore, the Human Relations movement put a more human face on the way administrators interacted with their workers. But make no doubt about it, the Human Relations Approach was still a closed systems model with the primary purpose of worker efficiency. In other words, managers treated their workers more humanely, gave them a larger role—at least prima facie—in decision-making, and created a climate of collegiality in order to get them to work better.

Critics claim that management's concern for workers is inauthentic in the Human Relations Approach. Rather, they say, these gentler and kinder practices are subtle ways to manipulate employees. It is as if the superiors are saying to their subordinates, "We'll make you happy as long as your work is excellent." It's the iron fist wrapped in the velvet glove.

From his own research Edward Greenberg stipulated, "In such a hierarchical system of supervision, workers are treated not as autonomous, rational, and responsible people but as persons to be watched, carefully managed, and compelled to work. Workers frequently mentioned that they were treated . . . as children."[15]

CONTEMPORARY HIGHER EDUCATION
GOVERNANCE MODELS

Let us now turn our attention to how these key attributes of closed systems thinking have manifested themselves in our contemporary institutions of higher learning.

The traditional or classical models of administration expect a great deal of control and authority by those in leadership positions.[16] In this largely quantitative world, scientific management seems to make sense—command and control, management-by-objective, solving problems by reductionist analysis of its parts, etc."[17]

Archon Fung was discouraged in his analysis of most contemporary governance systems. "In hierarchical models, accountability runs top-down, with central supervisors specifying methods and ends, and monitoring subordinates to see that they comply."[18] Hence the saying, when *you* expect, *you* must inspect.

In *Deepening Democracy*, Fung and coauthor Erik Wright stipulated that common practices of employee participation are less than truly empowering (akin to the Human Relations Approaches): "Empowered participatory decision-making can be contrasted with three more familiar methods of social choice: *command and control* by experts, *aggregative voting*, and *strategic negotiation* [all italics in original]."[19] The bottom line is these models are geared toward *managing workers*, not *leading professionals*.

If you were to ask most college presidents or senior cabinet members whether they practiced autocratic leadership, they would likely be offended. The majority would find themselves falling into one of two categories. Some would consider themselves firm, yet fair. They are paid to make the tough decisions and provide vision for their institutions. Their faculty and staff look to them for direction and a sense of security. They may say, "Leading faculty is like herding cats."

The second group includes "people" persons. Their style of leadership is that of a colleague and a "guide on the side." They help build a culture of family and community that inspires people to strive for optimal effectiveness. Administrators in both groups are most likely to practice situational leadership by altering their behavior depending on the circumstances.

Our universities are as rigidly structured as they were when they first adopted their industrial strictures. The hierarchy remains a de facto top-down governance and communication model wherein different silos, or divisions and departments, are aligned for efficiency and standardization. Division administrators sit atop these management pyramids. It is, however, not the premise of this book that bureaucratic structures and processes are wrong. Indeed, they are necessary. But, they should not be the proverbial "the tail wagging the dog."

At most colleges and universities, reporting directly to the president or chancellor are a series of vice presidents. Each of these cabinet members in turn have a series of directors or deans reporting to them. These administrators have specialized functions and corresponding responsibilities.

For instance, there are vice presidents for: academic affairs, administrative services, advancement and alumni relations, and enrollment management and marketing. Sub units for colleges/schools, library, technology, financial aid, registrar, student affairs, admissions, campus security, human resources, accounts payable, athletics, and so many others exist. Each of these units will have directors who supervise five to ten people with additional expertise.

Current decision-making practices are clearly impacted by closed systems thinking. Whether Classical Scientific Management or Human Relations orientation, these prototypical models share one thing in common when it comes to decision-making—both ultimate authority and responsibility rest in the office of the senior administration.

Organizations that use a Classical Scientific Management approach to management processes view decision-making as something explicitly under the purview of the administration. Everyone in the organization knows who makes the decisions; they do the hiring, and they do the firing—so to speak. It's the proverbial "iron fist" approach. Employees may even state, "Well, at least I know where the boss stands." The classical model is based on unilateral, linear decision-making processes—clear, clean, and precise.

If the administration and the *empowered* committee members disagree, the administration plays their trump card. Ultimately, the process is still the same—very linear and rationalistic with administration having the ultimate authority. It's the "iron fist wrapped in a velvet glove." Workers feel that at least with the old model they know they had little real input. The more modern approach leads workers to *feel* they are empowered at the outset. When they realize they are not *genuinely* empowered, they become disenfranchised and morale begins down the slippery precipice.

Faculty and staff are not the only ones alienated in the prototypical college organizational model. Students are at the bottom of the heap, and their level of influence is commensurate. Noam Chomsky bemoaned:

> Schools [are] institutions for indoctrination and for imposing obedience. Fare from creating independent thinkers, schools have always, throughout history, played an institutional role in a system of control and coercion. And once you are well educated, you have already been socialized in ways that support the power structure, which in turn rewards you immensely.[20]

Indeed, the vestiges of classical organizational thought and the human relations approach—both closed systems models—are so thoroughly engrained in our organizational psyche that we don't even question their impact on our work lives or governance structures. We simply take their presuppositions for granted as "the way things are"—our mimetic isomorphism—by doing or seeing things the way we were taught or enculturated.

The remainder of this chapter will provide the requisite framework for looking forward, in two ways. First, by looking through the lens of Critical Theory, we will dispel the myths of the need for command and control in traditional organizations and of the purported empowerment of the Human Relations Approach. Second, we will explore the postmodern approaches of open systems theories.

Critical Theory and Open Systems

> *People of discretion. Experts. I do not like experts. They are our jailors. I despise experts more than anyone on earth. . . . They solve nothing! They are servants of whatever system hires them. They perpetuate it. When we are tortured, we shall be tortured by experts. When we are hanged, experts will hang us. . . . When the world is destroyed, it will be destroyed not by madmen but by the sanity of its experts and the superior ignorance of its bureaucrats.[21] [Emphasis is mine]. ~~le Carre*

These lines of a Soviet scientist in John le Carre's novel, *The Russian House*, capture the essence of workers' deepening frustrations to those individuals who have authority over them. Unbeknownst to many contemporary administrative practitioners, this emotes the body of research called Critical Theory.

This research has remained on the fringe of administrative preparation programs because of its revolutionary bent and because of its lack of prescription. More succinctly, it's too radical with no perceived practical application for our leaders.

Critical Theory is just that. It's a theory (or better—a way of thinking) that is critical of the way things are. Critical theorists question everything. They question the status quo, power and authority structures, and even their own motivations. They look to truly empower workers. "Critical theory exposes abuses by elites and explores alternatives, more democratic and egalitarian models of organization."[22]

Proponents of Critical Theory desire bosses and workers alike to examine the status quo, to examine our assumptions of power relationships and of decision-making protocols, and to examine what we take for granted in our institutions.[23] In order to take a critical look at these assumptions, procedures, and relationships people need to enter processes of substantive dialogue. They must be allowed to express dissenting opinions without fear of subtle reprisal.

A low-level employee needs to be secure when challenging power and authority in their institution. During the Industrial Age, the management controlled with an iron fist. Everyone knew where they stood in the organization. The shift to the modern era of Human Relations Approaches has made the power dynamic more murky to see. According to Jermier:

> Contemporary mechanisms of control are often unobtrusive. . . . Although organizational theorists have long acknowledged that processes of control are integral to the way organizations operate there are reasons to believe that we have entered a new age in which the forms of control being used are more insidious and widely misunderstood.[24]

Therefore, the manipulation of Human Resources Management is unethical and tricks employees into feeling that they are empowered when, in fact, they are not.[25] Faculty and staff are asked to work on committees that carry out the vision of their superiors. Yet they have no real say in the vision. They set their goals, but the goals are from an allotment approved by administration. They are mentored into the ways of the system and told, "This is the way we do things around here." They become corporate clones embraced with group-think.

Employees have worked hard to get and maintain these jobs. They are compensated well and have very good health and retirement benefits. In other words, they have become comfortable, with too much to lose, to speak out against the group-think. When a subordinate voices dissidence, they could lose everything. So they keep quiet and don't verbalize their objections. This inaction is repeated every day across the organization. Workers have become victims of their own success.

Critical Theory asks employees and employers to question power relationships and motives of those making the decisions. Critical Theory not only criticizes the status quo but also looks to truly empower employees through democratic processes. In the words of Maxim Voronov and Peter Coleman, "Critical theory seeks to expose instances in which ideology constrains and oppresses certain groups while giving unfair advantage to others and to create more democratic workplaces."[26]

Critical Theory has taught us to be wary of hierarchical structures. There is little doubt that hierarchies and their corresponding bureaucracies have taken on a life of their own—a life that is choking out the life of the creative people who populate them. Furthermore, Critical Theory demands that those in power continually reflect upon their actions and policies to evaluate both their purposes and their effects.

Critical Theory has direct application to our institutions of higher learning. The most obvious impact is on our shared governance models and decision-making. The executive administration sets direction, creates expectations, and inspects the professionals' progress toward those expectations. When they cut budgets, senior administrators make decisions with "patriarchal compassion."

This statement may seem over the top; however, it is quite likely the reader has served on committees where the group had made a decision only to be overturned by the administration. It must be noted that these committees of educators typically truly can only make recommendations—they have no real authority. This is very routine, and it has created terrible morale issues among professors.

There is an alternative, however. Democratic decision-making processes and dialogue are central features to any system that chooses to provide a critical praxis and dialectic as defined by Paulo Freire.[27] Critical dialogue is the vehicle for practitioners to become aware of their condition, their promise, and how to get there.[28]

In other words, the professional workplace must offer a time and a place for faculty and staff to have honest and open dialogue. They must feel free to express themselves, to have transparent dialogue and come to reasoned conclusions together. They must be able to "speak truth to power."

Critical Theory thinking makes us question everything about our organizational structures and governance; but, these structures remain steadfast, today. We have made attempts to move from closed systems to open systems thinking, but it has been difficult to make the requisite changes. In a particularly poignant fashion, Fritjof Capra observed that

[s]ocial thought in the late nineteenth and early twentieth centuries was greatly influenced by positivism, a doctrine formulated by the social philosopher August Comte. Its assertions include the insistence that the social sciences should search for general laws of human behavior. . . . It is evident that the positivist framework is patterned after classical physics. Indeed, Auguste Comte, who introduced the term, "sociology," first called the scientific study "social physics." The major schools of thought in the early-twentieth-century sociology can be seen as attempts at emancipation from the positivist straitjacket.[29]

Whereas Closed Systems approaches were deterministic and used a machine metaphor, citizens in the country felt alienated by their own organizations. It was a time of questioning those in authority—vocally and sometimes physically. It was the era of the Vietnam War, Watergate, Civil Rights, and the sentiment was, "don't trust anyone over 30!"

This new postmodern view of organizations as natural systems is antipositivistic, nondeterministic, and operates with an ecological or jungle-like metaphor. It moved from the Newtonian to the Quantum. It doesn't subscribe to the notion that there is a linear way to understand problems and a purely rational way to administrate.

Rather, this movement born out of the 1960s believes that there is multiple and complex causation to most problems, that most decisions are not made with complete knowledge of all variables, and that organizations and their leaders are dramatically influenced by their institutions through a holistic lens and consider these systems as alive.

Like previous models, open systems theories arose in reaction to the shortcomings of its predecessors. "While alluring in their simplicity, mechanical concepts of school change run counter to the experience of most educators, who have learned to view all activity in schools as deeply human, subject to the baffling complexity that permeates most human endeavors."[30]

First, open systems hold that few simple cause-effect relationships exist within real-life systems. Effects are often far removed—in time and space—from their multiple causes. Second, top-down hierarchies, even though designed for efficiency, are ineffective and inefficient.

Human organizations should be considered dynamic living systems, unlike the rigid mechanical Closed Systems models that fail to interact with their environments. Whereas Closed Systems thinking took its cues from Newtonian physics, open systems thinking learned its lessons from the newer sciences, like quantum physics, ecology, biology, and chaos theory.[31]

Historian Jon Meacham quoted President Woodrow Wilson who stated that while America's democratic system appeared linear and clean, reality was different:

The trouble with the theory is that government is not a machine, but a living thing. . . . It falls, not under the theory of the universe, but under the theory of organic life. It is accountable to Darwin, not to Newton. It is modified by its environment, necessitated by its tasks, shaped to its functions by the sheer pressure of life. . . . Government is not a body of blind forces; it is a body of men . . . with a common task and purpose.[32]

Numerous scholars have shown us how we can apply these lessons to our organizations.[33] The new sciences tell us that, in natural systems, apparent chaos and disorder might actually be a new order unfolding. The very act of control and demand for homeostasis might actually harm or even kill the organization and certainly choke out innovation and growth.

At times we might need to allow the chaos to arise and the new order to unfold. But we must take a system-wide view.[34] Thus, we must avoid the compulsion to control and make quick decisions at times. Sometimes it is necessary to live with the uneasiness and allow the process to unfold.

Francis Newmann further explained not only that nonlinear models are most appropriate for governmental bodies, but that chaos should actually be used as a tool for dynamic growth. In his description of L. D. Kiel's work, Neumann posited,

Kiel wrote that public administration traditionally has focused on incremental or equilibrium models, which do not account for instances when dramatic whole-sale change can occur. He suggested that nonequilibrium processes appear to be more descriptive of the interactions of democratic societies, in which the political process brings external energy into the system and drives it far from equilibrium. It is the nonlinear process that allows the system to incorporate change within itself and to adapt to changing external environments. Kiel also suggested that agents can purposefully force change in organizations by energetically driving those organizations toward the points of chaotic thresholds. For example, he cited the situation in which Japanese executives intentionally drive their organizations to chaotic symmetry breaks. "Organizational upheaval is seen as positive. It creates instability, chaos, and potential for genuine qualitative change."[35]

The notion that our systems can be controlled and maintained at a state of equilibrium is erroneous. The tighter we try to squeeze our fist of control, the more the actual control or power oozes out between our fingers. We operate our organizations as if they were "tightly controlled systems, but again, that control is elusive. Human organizations operate more like loosely coupled systems." "Today's large organizations are disaggregating into loosely connected clusters of autonomous business units."[36]

Rhodes explained the false sense of power within the reality of "loosely coupled systems." "Note that power and control in each world [the world of planners and doers] is relatively meaningless since, in actuality, each remains relatively powerless to affect the system's results as long as they remain disconnected from each other."[37]

Proponents of the notion of loosely coupled systems believe that organizations are not nearly as tightly organized and managed in practice as one would believe by looking at work flow charts and organizational charts. Therefore, we need to create organizational models that embrace broader involvement and participation, rather than try to control it.

Further, being loosely coupled is an extremely important feature in professional organizations. Professionals often operate through their intuitions and experiences; they need to be allowed to have professional autonomy. Loosely coupled systems allow for flexibility and professional autonomy, and they allow for change to take place in relative isolation to the rest of the system.

The flip side to these positive attributes of loosely coupled systems is that change takes a great deal of time over the entire organization, and individuals have less control over the change process than they may wish or expect.

For boards of trustees and college presidents and senior administrators, the lessons from loosely coupled systems theory are important. We must fight the compulsion to control every aspect of the institution. The power we have *over* people is a misnomer. The power we have *with* people is more the reality. We may have *formal authority* over people, but our *power* comes *with* people. We must encourage and support professional autonomy with the smallest local units of our organizations and do all we can to build connections among these units and provide them with all information available.

Still, boards often feel they have no control, yet they have a vested interest in maintaining the status quo. As our institutions became larger, more complex, and greater expectations put upon them, administration felt they were losing control. Our leaders created a model for control and do everything to keep in control through their top-down bureaucratic hierarchies. Our leaders must fight this tendency.

As we have learned, bureaucratic hierarchies clearly have their critical limitations. These issues range from being unable to deliver the pragmatism for which they were designed to serving as dehumanizing places to work. And for the purpose of this book, bureaucratic hierarchies are not congruent with our country's foundational democratic principles, as we will explore in the chapter 3. Well-renowned political analyst for CNN and the *Washington Post*, Fareed Zakaria reported, "Historically, unchecked centralization has been the enemy of liberal democracy."[38]

So, the siloed, top-down, classical model of Closed Systems organizations is antiquated and ineffectual. But, a more professional, realistic, and natural open systems model is revealed, again. It is the democratic organization, and it is the focus of the remainder of this book. First, let's rejoin Sam along her journey.

SAM—HERE I STAND; I CAN DO NO OTHER

Sam often thought of this famous quote of Martin Luther as he confronted the bureaucracy of the church: "Here I stand; I can do no other." It was the kind of quote on leadership she often used to keep her going when times got rough. She was thinking of Martin Luther's solitary fight against the formal church hierarchy when there was a knock at her door.

It was Professor David Sinclair of the history department and a renowned scholar of the U.S. Constitution. "Dr. Sabbon, might I have a few moments of your time?"

"For you, Dr. Sinclair, it is always my pleasure. What can I do for you, today?"

Dr. Sinclair sat down and began and looked directly at her with his gray eyes. While he was a gentleman, Dr. Sinclair's stare was known to intimidate people, certainly his students.

Each fall semester I have a couple of guest speakers come to my freshmen U.S. History class to speak about a particular topic. I have a corporate CEO speak about governance in the industrial sector, and I have had your predecessor speak about governance in higher education. Likewise, I have Professor Sheinglen do an overview of comparative democratic governance structures in Europe. So, with all that said, I'm wondering if you might be able to share your thoughts with my class, this semester.

"Oh my, David, I'm thrilled and terrified all at the same time," came Sam's uncomfortable response. "I mean, what a wonderful idea, but I don't know what I would say. I don't know anything about the history of shared governance, just my own experience," she said with a regrettable smile.

"Precisely, that's why you would be a tremendous speaker. The students don't need a dry didactic presentation; they need to be engaged. They need to hear real-life governance. Your experiences as both a former faculty senator and as a current administrator would make the concepts meaningful."

Sam listened intently and was quiet for a moment. Then, she agreed. "I'll do it!"

David and Sam spent the next ten minutes talking about logistics and details. She would have forty-five minutes for one class period next month. She knew she had her work cut out. As Dr. Sinclair was leaving, Sam said, "Oh, David, I would love to sit in on your corporate guest's presentation!"

"No problem, Sam! Karl was my college roommate. I'll give him a heads-up, but I know he will love it."

Sam had a huge sigh of relief on her face, and then David added, "And, I'll invite him to your presentation." The smile fell from her face.

At home, Sam reflected back upon the conversation she had four hours earlier with Dr. Sinclair. She started to make some notes to herself about what she needed to cover. But, one salient point mentioned by her colleague kept nagging at her. "The students don't need a dry didactic presentation." Certainly that was true, but this was going to be a challenge.

Sam's to-do list included history and purpose of shared governance, examples of shared governance, her experiences with shared governance, concerns, and, most importantly, how to make the presentation engaging! These thoughts leapt through her mind as she stood at her kitchen sink where a load of dishes, two days' worth, sat waiting for her. Sam wondered how mothers with children could manage both a professional career and raising a family. She felt a twinge of shame thinking of her sister Leslie who had a daughter and a son while at the same time worked on her MBA. and started a small business.

It was Monday morning. Meng Xiong and President Davis were just wrapping up their one-hour dialogue with the two HEMetrics consultants assigned to Founders University. Meng would serve as the Strategic Plan Steering Committee chair. Drs. Thompson and Mason of HEMetrics introduced themselves to the president's cabinet of vice presidents. Geoff Thompson outlined the agenda for the day's activities:

8:00–9:00	Meet with President Davis and Chair Xiong,
9:00–10:00	Meet with President's Cabinet—all Vice Presidents,
10:00–10:20	Break,
10:20–11:20	Meet with faculty senate executive committee,
11:30–1:00	Lunch with President Davis, Chair Xiong, and board of trustees executive committee,
1:00–2:30	Open Forum with interested faculty and staff,
2:30–3:00	Consultant prep time, and
3:00–3:30	HEMetrics debrief with President Davis and Chair Xiong.

Consultants Thompson and Mason spent nearly half an hour detailing for the vice presidents HEMetric's approach to strategic planning, timelines, and the vice presidents' roles. The remainder of the hour served as a listening session as the consultants heard the senior staff's big ideas, concerns and threats, strengths and weaknesses, and opportunities. Much of the conversation focused on "the way things are," competition, needs for funding support and staffing, and improvements for infrastructure including facilities and technology. The consultants would have similar conversations with the other groups throughout the day.

Sam made a mental note that no fora were scheduled for students, alumni, or external groups. She also noted that there was a forum for faculty and staff, but no special session, like a focus group, for them similar to the one the senior administration was having. "Maybe that would be impossible to pull off," she thought to herself. That was better than the alternative of not really caring for significant input. Sam was also curious what the trustees, faculty, and staff would have to say.

While President Davis, Dr. Xiong, and the consultants met with the executive committee of the board, VPAF Hutchins held an ad hoc meeting with the other vice presidents to elaborate on potential budget cuts. He explained to his colleagues that less-than-expected, tuition-based revenues along with unforeseen insurance increases would likely necessitate budget cuts. President Davis asked Mr. Hutchins to put together scenarios of 5 percent and 10 percent decreases from the present operating budget. These scenarios were now shared with the council members and to be shredded after the meeting concluded.

Henry Hutchins concluded his presentation: "President Davis and I agree that across-the-board cuts are best in order to spread the pain. Hopefully, we won't need to make the cuts deeper than 5%. By next Friday, I need you to submit to me reworked budgets showing both these scenarios. We won't micromanage your cuts; we just need to see the bottom-line."

Outright angst filled the room. Advancement VP Peter Gabrielse was the first to enter the conversation. "This is about impossible, Henry! Both the fiscal and the academic years are well underway, and the largest portions of our expenditures have been front-loaded. In other words, most purchases have already been made. With 5%, and especially with 10% cuts, the rest of my budget will be significantly impacted. It's not 10% of the total budget; it's 10% of the total from the remaining budget!"

Henry paused for just a second. "To be most fiscally prudent, you should spread out your expenditures equally across the year, Peter."

Peter's mouth fell open with a combination of anger and disbelief. There was a pregnant pause that caused Sam much discomfort. She finally added, "Henry, I don' think across-the-board cuts are fair and appropriate. They may be equitable, but they are not equal."

"What do you mean, Sam?" followed Henry.

"Well, they are equitable in that everyone has the same percentage cut, but the impact of the cuts on different units have greater or lesser impact on the institution. Let me elaborate. In my units, I won't make equitable cuts. I'm going to need to cut some areas/accounts more than others. I'm not going to cut, for example, everyone's salaries by 10% which would be equitable. Rather, I might have to cut one person in one program."

"Like I said, Sam, we are not going to micromanage."

"True, Henry, but shouldn't you and Lloyd not focus on equity as much as targeted areas?" came Sam's retort.

The other vice presidents affirmed these thoughts and shared other concerns and ideas, as well. Henry concluded the meeting by saying that he would debrief President Davis in the afternoon and that the institution had weathered these storms in the past. In the meantime, this discussion was to be held in confidence: "No reason to rile up the college and get a lot of faculty panicking."

Sam was rather dismayed about Henry's closing comments. Sure, senior administration needed the space and time to consider plans, but what about transparency and shared decision-making? It seemed demeaning to think that faculty would "panic." Is that way of thinking necessary, or is it an antiquated way of treating professionals?

In any case, Sam needed to run back to her office to eat a quick granola bar and some grapes while she reviewed her email to see if any pressing issues came up over the last couple of hours. The only item that raised her eyebrows was an email from the editor of the school newspaper—Shelley Newcombe. Shelley wanted to interview Sam. Sam replied that she would be available tomorrow morning, but for now she had to run to meet with the faculty senate executive committee.

The executive committee met in a small conference room in the School of Education, as President Norman Evenson was a special education professor. Other members included Professor McQuinlan (vice president), assistant professor of health sciences Tisha Tucker (secretary), and associate professor of business administration Abe Samuelson (parliamentarian). Sam was a special guest at this meeting.

The agenda only had two topics. Under Standing Business: Assembly Plans (Tucker), and under New Business: Committee Reconstitution (McQuinlan and Sabbon). The meeting had no distinctive formality; rather, it was a congenial and informal discussion among colleagues.

The conference room was an eclectic menagerie of furniture from different generations. The conference room table had to have been purchased in the 1970s. Two different types of chairs surrounded this huge table which bore various cuts and scuffs of bygone decades. Event posters and meeting notices blotted the walls—some of these were posted last year. And, a new large screen television monitor sat on a corner table with cords going in various directions.

President Evenson started, "I hope we can make this a quick meeting, because I have an advisee who needs to see me in twenty minutes. The first order of business is the schedule for the Assembly next month. Tisha, can you tell us where we stand with our guest speaker?"

"Sure, Norm. Professor of Humanities at Belkamp College Misty Cunningham has agreed to speak to the entire Assembly. Her topic will be: Re-envisioning Learning Communities through Old-Fashioned European Salons. She will speak for 45-minutes and will follow with an hour seminar for interested faculty."

"That's terrific, Trish!" exclaimed Norman Evenson. Everyone nodded in agreement with a sense of self-congratulations. The television monitor all of a sudden lit up, flickered, and then went dark again. Everyone looked at each other as if the room was haunted.

Norm continued, "Do we have any announcements to make?"

Trish looked at her notes and responded, "We need to make certain everyone submits their early-alert reports to the Student Learning Center." Sam nodded vigorously in agreement.

"One other thing," continued Abe Samuelson, "we need to start preparing for advising for the spring semester."

"Good. Okay, let's get to our last order of business," Norm responded in quick order. With that, he turned to Patrick and gestured for his vice president to introduce the final topic.

"Yeah, Norm. Dr. Sabbon and I had a conversation recently that is truly of interest to me and is quite thought-provoking." Patrick went on to tell his executive colleagues about the conversation he and Sam had had earlier.

With that, Norman turned to Sam with a squint as if to say, "I've heard these kinds of ideas before, they get people fired up, lots of work and energy are expelled, and then nothing gets done since senior administration kills it." Well, at least that's what Sam inferred from Norman's demeanor.

So, she decided to jump right in. "Thank you, Norm. Really, Patrick captured it. Through nobody's fault, I think faculty senates across the country have lost their focus, their voice, if you will. Now, they go through the motions and make occasional proclamations, and each year looks like the last. I want the faculty to get its voice back, to push the institution. I don't know . . . maybe I'm just looking back to our youth where universities used to be that place where new thinking was generated—the place where you wanted to be." Sam wondered if she was coming across too forcefully.

"That's a by-gone era, Sam," came Norman's response. "But, I appreciate your sincerity. What do you propose?"

Sam had no idea. She was actually just hoping for affirmation from her faculty colleagues. "I'm not sure. Maybe I could speak at the next faculty meeting—not the Assembly, but the next Senate meeting. I could see if anyone is interested in exploring this idea with me." Sam was relieved she thought of this response.

"Very good, Sam. Trish, please put Dr. Sabbon on our next meeting agenda. Now, I have to run to meet with my advisee. See you all next week." With that said, Norm closed the meeting. Patrick and Sam walked out together not knowing what to expect.

NOTES

1. Eldridge Cleaver, *Soul on Ice* (New York: Dell Publishing, 1968), 84.

2. Perry Rettig, *Reframing Decision Making in Education: Democratic Empowerment of Teachers and Parents* (Lanham, MD: Rowman & Littlefield, 2016). Much of this chapter is drawn upon the work from this earlier book, as well as that from: Perry Rettig, *Quantum Leaps in School Leadership* (Lanham, MD: Rowman & Littlefield, 2002). As an interesting aside, Bowen and Tobin wrote of Taylor's involvement in higher education governance:

> A more controversial effort to make universities "business-like" was launched by President Henry Pritchett of the CFAT in 1909, when he commissioned Morris L. Cooke, a protégé of the scientific management guru Frederick Taylor, to study academic and industrial efficiency. Cooke sought to measure faculty efficiency in terms of student hours of instruction and, more generally, recommended removing faculty from all aspects of governance, which he thought should be "the exclusive prerogative of management" (William Bowen and Eugene Tobin, *Locus of Authority: The Evolution of Faculty Roles in the Governance of Higher Education.* (Princeton, NJ: Princeton University Press, 2015), 55.

3. Robert Owens, *Organizational Behavior in Education: Adaptive Leadership and School Reform* (New York: Pearson Allyn & Bacon, 2004), 83.

4. Reginald Green, *Practicing the Art of Leadership: A Problem-Based Approach to Implementing the ISLLC Standards* (Upper Saddle River, NJ: Merrill Prentice Hall, 2001), 53.

5. Peter Block, *Stewardship: Choosing Service over Self-Interest* (San Francisco: Berrett-Koehler, 1996), 8.

6. Teresa Harrison, "Designing the Post-Bureaucratic Organization: Toward Egalitarian Organizational Structure," *Australian Journal of Communication* 19 (2) (1992), 14–29. For an interesting description of the history of organizational theory, please read this excellent article.

7. Peter Blau, *The Organization of Academic Work* (New York: Wiley, 1973), 383.

8. James G. March and Johan P. Olsen, *Democratic Governance* (New York: The Free Press, 1995), 79.

9. Charles Heckscher, "Defining the Post-Bureaucratic Type," In Charles Heckscher and Anne Donnellon eds, *The Post-Bureaucratic Organization: New Perspectives on Organizational Change* (Thousand Oaks, CA: Sage, 1994), 37.

10. Owens, *Organizational Behavior in Education*, 2004.

11. Mihalyi Csikszentmihalyi, *Flow: The Psychology of Optimal Experience* (New York: Harper Collins, 1990), 78.

12. Francis Neumann, Jr., "Organizational Structures to Match the New Information-Rich Environments: Lessons from the Study of Chaos," *Public Productivity and Management Review* 21 (September 1997), 90.

13. Owens, *Organizational Behavior in Education*, 90–91.

14. Ibid., 93.

15. Edward Greenberg, *Workplace Democracy: The Political Effects of Participation* (Ithaca, NY: Cornell University Press, 1986), 45.

16. Rettig, *Reframing Decision Making in Education*, 2.

17. L. Rhodes, "Connecting Leadership and Learning," In *A Planning Paper Developed for the American Association of School Administrators National Center for Connected Learning* (April 1997), 16.

18. Archon Fung, *Empowered Participation: Reinventing Urban Democracy* (Princeton, NJ: Princeton University Press, 2004), 69.

19. Archon Fung and Erik Wright, *Deepening Democracy: Institutional Innovations in Empowered Participatory Governance* (London, England: Verso, 2003). On page 19 these authors provided further detail about the methods associated with all three of these "choices"

> In [command and control], power is invested in managers, bureaucrats, or other specialists. While such experts may engage in deliberative practices among themselves, their discussions are insulated from popular participation. On the other hand, in aggregate voting the administrator will allow participation. Individual group members are permitted to vote on a variety of issues, then an algorithm such as majority rule selects a single option for the whole group. Still, invariably, it is the administrator who decides which issues make it on the agenda to receive employee consideration.

20. Noam Chomsky, *Chomsky: On Miseducation* (Lanham, MD: Rowman & Littlefield, 2000), 16.

21. Le Carre in Howard Zinn. This quote was cited in Howard Zinn, *Declarations of Independence: Cross-Examining American Ideology* (New York: Harper Collins, 1990). Zinn referenced J. Le Carre's *The Russian House* (Knopf. 1989), 6. Page 207. Zinn went on to express the radical nature of Critical Theory. In his words, "If those in charge of our society—politicians, corporate executives, and owners of press and television—can dominate our ideas, they will be secure in their power. They will not need soldiers patrolling the streets. We will control ourselves." (2)

22. Russ Marion, *Leadership in Education: Organizational Theory for the Practitioner* (Upper Saddle River, NJ: Merrill Prentice Hall, 2002).

23. L. Beyer, "The Value of Critical Perspectives in Teacher Education," *Journal of Teacher Education* 52 (2) (March/April 2001).

24. J. Jermier, "Critical Perspectives on Organizational Control," *Administrative Science Quarterly* 43 (1998), 235.

25. Maxim Voronov and Peter T. Coleman, "Beyond the Ivory Towers: Organizational Power Practices and a 'Practical' Critical Post-modernism," *The Journal of Applied Behavioral Science* 39 (2) (June 2003), 172.

> For example, critical theorists have asserted that the quality of life, worker satisfaction, and participative management concerns expressed by human relations scholars are little more than clever ways to quell any potential for employee resistance and to increase managerial control over organizations. They argue, for example, that feeling empowered is not the same thing as being empowered. Choosing one of the limited options for getting the work done, in which both the agenda and the methods are defined by the management, is not empowering. Whereas more traditional management scholars take the managerial point of view, critical theorists take the employee perspective. The goal of critical theorists is to expose systems of domination and to reform organizations to create new organizational arrangements, which would be free of exploitive power arrangements and distorted communication. Voronov and Coleman continue, "Those in the lower echelons of the hierarchy often are 'duped' by those at the top into believing that they are empowered, although in reality they are still being controlled from above and by each other through ideology or disciplinary power." (176)

26. Voronov and Coleman, "Beyond the Ivory Towers," 173.

27. Paulo Freire, *Pedagogy of the Oppressed* (New York: Continuum, 1970). For a most insightful examination of Critical Theory's application to the educational enterprise, the reader is encouraged to read Freire.

28. D. Comstock, "A Method for Critical Research," In E. Bredo and W. Feinberg, eds. *Knowledge and Values in Social and Educational Research* (Philadelphia: Temple University Press, 1982), 382.

29. Fritjof Capra, *The Hidden Connections: A Science for Sustainable Living* (New York: Anchor Books, 2004), 75.

30. John Clarke, *Personalized Learning* (Lanham, MD: Rowman & Littlefield, 2002), 309.

31. Rettig, *Quantum Leaps in School Leadership.*

32. Jon Meacham, *The Soul of America: The Battle for Our Better Angels* (New York: Random House, 2018), 36. Quoting President Woodrow Wilson.

33. Capra, *The Hidden Connections,* 2004.

34. John H. Clarke, "Growing High School Reform: Planting the Seeds of Systemic Change," *NASSP Bulletin* (April 1999), 4.

35. Neumann, Jr., "Organizational Structures to Match the New Information-Rich Environments: Lessons from the Study of Chaos," 95.

36. William Halal, *The New Management: Bringing Democracy and Markets Inside Organizations* (San Francisco: Berrett-Koehler, 1998), 83.

37. Rhodes, "Connecting Leadership and Learning," 15.

38. Fareed Zakaria, *The Future of Freedom: Illiberal Democracy at Home and Abroad* (New York: W. W. Norton & Company, 2003), 105.

Chapter 3

What If?

Here, I stand; I can do no other.

Martin Luther

This book is about change—about reimagining original intent. It's about reestablishing organizational structures and administrative practices and even culture in order to be more congruent with the democratic principles by which our country was founded—yet principles that have been left at the front door of our institutions of higher learning.

But this book is even more about changing our perceptions of what it means to be a professional within our organizations. It's about challenging the roles of the board, senior administration, faculty, staff, and even students in shared governance. By examining with fresh eyes our originating democratic principles through the lens of Critical Theory, we can reconceptualize a new approach to shared governance—one that maintains ageless integrity yet may be more nimble, natural, and adaptable.

We have come to assume that our institutions must have rigid, static structures—our mimetic isomorphism. However, if we look to the newer sciences we learn that natural systems have fluid structures that respond to the environment. "The defining characteristic of an autopoietic system is that it undergoes continual structural changes while preserving its weblike pattern of organization."[1]

These dynamic structures allow for the system to respond to the ever-changing demands of the environment—to survive. Yet, we spend a tremendous amount of money, energy, and time attempting to maintain equilibrium, and we don't even realize we're choking our colleges and universities.

Just how do these postmodern, natural concepts relate to our current, yet antiquated, organizations? Heckscher clearly elucidates the current affairs of our organizations, but then he gives a glimpse of how we can begin to change our organizations in this postmodern world:

> There is a growing sense that effective organization change has its own dynamic, a process that cannot simply follow strategic shifts and that is longer and subtler than can be managed by any single leader. It is generated from the insights of many people trying to improve the whole, and it accumulates, as it were, over long periods. Dramatic moments of "revolutionary" transformation are only a small piece of it, and often are the most effective way to bring about change. If this is true—and there is much reason to believe it is—the bureaucratic structures are not the most effective ones for managing the process.[2]

In addition, and related to Open Systems thinking, Heckscher, Eisenstat, and Rice stated, "When people agree to enter a dialogue, they know that the power relations will change—and they are not sure how. This is an example of 'bootstrapping.' . . . They cannot see the advantages of a higher-order system until they have entered it, but they fear it until they have understood it."[3] democratic organizations will threaten these leaders.

Educators might have become victims of their own success and fearful of requisite change. While it may have taken decades to happen, faculty and staff now get paid decent salaries, and their fringe-benefits packages are quite good. They now have too much to lose. If they "rock the boat" their jobs or advancement opportunities may be put in jeopardy.

Many colleges are no longer offering tenure, so that safety net is gone. When you don't have much, it's not such a big deal to risk it all. When you are comfortable, you risk a great deal by pushing the system to its bifurcation point. These professionals have become victims of their own success. Thus, people are afraid to begin the change process because they are afraid they may very well lose the position of their status (with associated pay and benefits), and they have no idea what they might end up doing when they come through the other end of the change process.

Management of the change process is designed theoretically to be very clean and precise in our modern organizations. In the words of Capra, "The principles of classical management theory have become so deeply ingrained in the ways we think about organizations that for most managers the design of formal structures, linked by clear lines of communication, coordination, and control, has become almost second nature. We shall see that this largely unconscious embrace of the mechanistic approach to management is one of the main obstacles to organizational change today."[4]

This traditional model for directing change is invariably instigated from the top—by design. As posited by Wells and Picou, "Innovation tends to be structured either directly or indirectly by people, especially administrators, who are in the necessary power positions to bring about changes."[5] These managers are operating by assumptions that they were taught—they are following the rules for creating change. This top-down approach to creating change, however, is often not embraced by the workers. Again, this is an example of our mimetic isomorphism.

Without employee support, however, full and sustained implementation is not likely. Again, Wells and Picou states, "It seems then, that some sort of antagonistic cooperation between faculty and administration is a necessary condition for successful educational innovation."[6] This antagonism is the practical flaw in classical methods of creating change and traditional strategic planning.

Earlier, we learned from Francis Neumann, Jr. that modern organizations assume that their systems operate in an environment of equilibrium. However, Neumann—citing Kiel—explained that postmodern organizations live in a different environment:

> [Kiel] suggested that nonequilibrium processes appear to be more descriptive of the interactions of *democratic* [emphasis added] societies, in which the political processes brings external energy into the system and drives it far from stability. It is the nonlinear process that allows the system to incorporate change within itself and to adapt to changing external environments. Kiel also suggested that agents can purposefully force change in organizations toward the points of chaotic thresholds.[7]

Thus, while administrative leaders may not be able to control system change, comprehensive administrative reform is a most plausible strategy for "democratic institutional adaptation."[8]

MOVING TOWARD DEMOCRACY

It is the contention of this book that in order for our institutions of higher learning to survive and flourish, fundamental organizational changes must occur. Through the lens of Critical Theory, we should reexamine our founding democratic principles for direction. Yet our contemporary operating procedures are far from democratic, and we ourselves will most likely fight this change.

March and Olsen noted, "The development of bureaucratic expertise, position, and isolation becomes an oligarchic threat to democracy."[9] So, our bureaucratic structures have become anathema to democratic governance. But, at the same time, there are critics and concerns with such governing principles. Let us in turn examine these concerns of democratic governance.

Not only are there perceived hurdles in both public and private colleges and universities, but even the corporate sector shares these obstacles to reform. In his study of cooperative enterprises in the United States, Edward Greenberg highlighted this concern:

> The paradox of enterprise authoritarianism operating within a formally demo-cratic political system is particularly marked in the United States where sur-prisingly few advances have been made toward democracy in the workplace and the distribution and practice of formal democratic rights and liberties are theoretically the most wide-spread. As a condition of earning a living, Ameri-can workers must give up their accustomed rights and privileges of citizenship upon crossing the threshold of the factory gate or office door. Within the busi-ness firm, the rights of free speech, free association, election of leadership, and general control of collective policy—so central to most definitions of the demo-cratic polity—are not generally considered to be in effect.[10]

Even more, administrators and employees alike have grave concerns about making our work organizations democratic. Change in power structures is invariably a concern when it comes to empowering employees. Managers may feel that they will lose their prestige and even their jobs—that they will no longer be needed in these postmodern organizations.[11]

Management will claim that as they move into democratic organizations, they retain all their former responsibility yet lose their previous auton-omy[12] and power.[13] Allowing for fuller employee participation could even cause employees to begin to question management's legitimacy to claim authority.[14]

Workers and staff can also see concerns about perceived shifts in power; they may well believe in the management's move to empower employees as disingenuous. In other words, they have experienced the manipulations of Human Relations Approaches to employee empowerment.

In fact, it has been noted earlier that moves to apparent democratization of the workplace may indeed be manipulations by administration to gain even more control. Kezar and Holcombe explained, "[S]hared leadership was pri-marily a rhetorical strategy used by vertical leaders to give the impression of inclusion and collaboration."[15]

According to John Smyth, "The basic argument is that moves towards devolution, in most cases, are not fundamentally about grassroots democratic reform of education aimed at giving schools and their communities more power—rather, they are about precisely the reverse, namely, the intensifica-tion of central control, while seeming to be otherwise."[16] In other words, administration's apparent movement toward democratic empowerment may actually be more about appearances of shared governance while at the same time maintaining real control.

This Critical Theory perspective of insidious manipulation views management's "giving away power" as their way to get employees to do what management really wanted all along, by letting workers believe they are empowered when they truly are not. In regard to how employees are permitted to speak freely, most often their freedom is limited.

Noted historian Howard Zinn explained, "The problem with free speech in the United States is not with the *fact* [emphasis in original] of access, but with the degree of it. There is *some* access to dissident views, but these are pushed to the corner."[17]

A very legitimate concern with new democratic structures is that, because that's all they know, the oppressed will become the oppressors once they have power.[18] As pointed out by postmodernists, institutionalizing a new order might simply lead to new power arrangements and produce new inequalities. "Postmodernism is suspicious of all grand narratives and points out the potential for domination inherent even in the best of intentions,"[19] according to Voronov and Coleman.

In a concurring opinion, Fareed Zakaria exclaimed, "The tendency for a democratic government to believe it has absolute sovereignty (that is, power) can result in the centralization of authority, often by extraconstitutional means and with grim results."[20] Hence the maxim: *Power corrupts, and absolute power corrupts absolutely.*

Besides issues related to power, employers and employees alike have other concerns about democratic models. First and foremost, people are afraid of an organizational bifurcation where the system will either leap into a higher complexity—democratization of the workplace—or fall into chaos and die. Again, in the words of Voronov and Coleman, "Emancipation may result in a profound confusion, general distrust, and depression."[21]

Chaos can lead to another fear—the fear of vice. "Corruption thrives on disorganization, the absence of stable relationships among groups and of reorganized patterns of authority."[22] In a most erudite insight, Bachrach and Botwinick explained, "The idea of democracy can continue to function as a creatively disruptive force in the polity, especially in provoking protest and struggle against the contradiction between oligarchical rule in the workplace and the idea of democracy."[23]

Pragmatic concerns also swirl around democratization of the workplace. It has been expressed that democracies are inefficient.[24] From concerns of inefficiency, people also worry that democratic decision-making takes too much time. John Smyth explained that in the K-12 setting, "A great deal of teachers can be diverted away from the primary task of teaching and learning. The energies of the principal can also be diverted away from being the educational leader."[25]

Gamson and Levin cite "four problems in democratic decision-making that appear frequently enough to constitute common issues." These are: the legitimate exercise of authority; obtaining accountability from members; the productive use of conflict; and, the productive use of meetings.[26]

Indeed, there are numerous concerns as we look to move toward more democratic organizations. These concerns could be enumerated as follows:

- *Appearance of democracy*: Are these changes real, or are they a disingenuous manipulation by leadership to keep employees in line?
- *Degree of democracy*: Associated with the first concern is the question about how much voice will be given to the employees. In what areas and to what extent will they be able to participate?
- *Power structures*: Will old power structures simply be replaced by new power structures? Will management lose power? Will new forms of oppression be created?
- *Accountability and representation*: Who will be held accountable for decisions and results? Who is in charge? Will all groups be represented and given voice?
- *Efficiency*: How much time will democratic decision-making take? Will the process be efficient and productive?

Even if we are successful in fully implementing genuine participatory decision-making systems, we need to continually examine and audit these systems, processes, and structures. "Ultimately, each presumed case of workplace democratization needs careful scrutiny with respect to such dimensions as (a) the range of issues about which participants may speak, (b) the extent of actual influence by employees through their exercise of voice, and (c) the levels of their hierarchy at which meaningful voice is possible."[27]

Chapter 4 will revisit these concerns in the context of higher education and conceptualize a modified system of checks and balances and processes to mitigate these concerns. For now, let us turn our attention to key democratic principles.

DEMOCRATIC PRINCIPLES

"There is an unmistakable contradiction between the democratic values of freedom and independence and the colonial and patriarchal strategies used to manage our organizations."[28] Peter Block used these words to alert us to the incongruence between our country's democratic ideals and the everyday practices of our places of employment. But what precisely are the democratic values and principles that we hold so dear? Specifically, which values and principles can we relate directly to our colleges for shared governance?

Can democratic principles even be applied to our work environments? Edward Greenberg is emphatic in this affirmation. "Complex modern institutions can be successfully operated on a basis of democratic, egalitarian, and nonhierarchical principles even in an environment that is hostile to such principles in the workplace in the United States."[29]

Before we examine our country's founding documents, it is important that we consider a few of the core values that helped the framers put these seminal works together.[30] Five essential core values that we can relate to our workplaces are liberty, common good, justice, equality, and diversity. *Liberty* refers to personal freedom and "the right to a free flow of information and ideas, open debated and [the] right to assembly." For the workplace, the *common good* means that each worker is committed to work with their fellow employees for "the greater benefit of all."

For *justice* to exist, workers "should be treated fairly . . . in the gathering of information and making of decisions." *Equality* requires that "there should be no class hierarchy sanctioned by law" and inordinate economic inequality. Finally, in order to ensure *diversity*, we need a "variety in culture and ethnic background, race, lifestyle, and belief."[31]

It would appear that these fundamental beliefs have as their core tenets the belief in honesty, openness, and fairness. Workers must be treated fairly, open communication and decision-making are essential, and processes must be transparent.

According to constitutioncenter.org, there are eight constitutional principles (enumerated in the following paragraphs).[32] These principles are: rule of law, separation of powers, representative government, checks and balances, individual rights, freedom of religion, federalism, and civilian control of the military. The first four are most striking for the discussion at hand. For the *rule of law*, it would seem apparent that all members of an organization should be held to the same rules, regulations, and standards, and that they be treated fairly.

For the government, the *separation of powers* doctrine provides for the legislative, executive, and judicial branches so that these powers "should be exercised by different institutions in order to maintain the limitations placed upon them." The doctrine of the separation of powers is designed so that no one person or body has too much power.

In the words of noted historian Samuel Huntington, "The passion of the Founding Fathers for the division of power, for setting ambition against ambition, for creating a constitution with a complicated systems of balances exceeding that of any other, is, of course, well known. Everything is bought at a price, however, and . . . one apparent price of the division of power is government inefficiency."[33] As our higher education systems currently stand, one might consider that we do have some separation of powers, at least framed on paper.

At our colleges and universities, we have the executive administration, boards of trustees/regents, and faculty senates. The balance of power between these three groups, while historically spelled out in bylaws and articles of incorporation, has become blurred and are not balanced. A democratic model will be reenvisioned in chapter 4—where we will set forth a structure for the balance of powers and a system of checks and balances. While Huntington mentioned democratic models are inefficient, our current hierarchical systems are no models of efficiency!

In the workplace, *representative government* starts with the premise that the workers represent themselves, either directly or indirectly, through elected representation. The critical point is that the workers are truly empowered. In the doctrine of *checks and balances*, "the powers given to the different branches of government should be balanced, that is roughly equal, so that no branch can completely dominate the others."

"Branches of government are also given powers to check the power of other branches." In higher education, it has become apparent that the executive "branch" has an inordinate amount of power, and there exists no judicial branch, of course. In a strikingly similar tone to that of Samuel Huntington, contemporary historian Fareed Zakaria states,

> Constitutionalism, as it was understood by its greatest eighteenth-century exponents, such as Montesquieu and Madison, is a complicated system of checks and balances designed to prevent the accumulation of power and the abuse of office. . . . Various groups must be included and empowered because, as Madison explained, "ambition must be made to counteract ambition."[34]

The reader can determine for their own particular circumstance to what degree their institution balances or limits power and provides for a system of checks and balances. The dual doctrines of the separation of powers and of checks and balances are critical to rethinking the ways we operate our colleges and universities. So, more time and detail will be spent with them in chapter 4.

It is time for us to now turn our attention to some of the details in our country's founding documents. In our nation's constitution, we find several articles and sections to be applicable to the workplace.

The first half of the second paragraph to the Declaration of Independence reads,

> *We hold these truths to be self-evident, that all men are created equal, that they are endowed by their Creator with certain inalienable Rights, that among these are Life, Liberty, and the pursuit of Happiness. That to secure these rights, Governments are instituted among Men, deriving their just powers from the consent of the governed.*

There are at least two lessons we can take away from these introductory sentences.

First, we should, without question, understand that all individuals are created equal. While we may not have equal training, knowledge, skills, responsibilities, and the like, we should all be valued as equal. We could quibble that an important distinction is that the original document clearly states that "all men are *created* equal," and that because of our roles and responsibilities, we are no longer equal at work. The point is that each of us brings special value to our organizations and needs to be treated with dignity and respect.

Second, our institutions are developed and maintained by people, and the people who are designated with power and authority derive that power and authority from the employees or constituent groups. This latter point is crucial for the discussion at hand. Our leaders are given their authority, not by some impersonal legalistic or rational agreements, but directly from the workers and their communities.

Numerous lessons can be learned from the U.S. Constitution. In Article I, Section 1, we learn that "all legislative Powers herein granted shall be vested in a Congress of the United States, which shall consist of a Senate and a House of Representatives." Sections 2 and 3 of Article I explicate how members of Congress—the House of Representatives and the Senate, respectively, will be apportioned and elected.

Appropriate details will be covered in chapter 4 of this book. From Article I, Section 1, however, we may interpret that the faculty and staff (and even students) are represented by people whom they choose.

The two types of representation—House of Representatives and Senate—allow for a balance of powers. In other words, it provides for both majority rule and protection of the rights of the minority. Section 4 states that "the Congress shall assemble at least once in every Year."

Section 5 stipulates, "Each House shall keep a Journal of its Proceedings, and from time to time publish the same." From these two sections we learn that our representative bodies need to meet to deal with the organization's business on at least an annual basis and that this business must be recorded for all to see; this will provide the requisite transparency to deliberations.

Section 6 speaks to compensation of representatives and that they are forbidden to concurrently hold two offices. Section 7 is reserved to discussion of procedures for bills to become laws. Here, we learn that bills must be passed by both houses of Congress and the president. If the president (executive) vetoes a bill, it can be overturned by a two-thirds majority vote by the House.

Again, we can apply lessons from this section of the Constitution to our institutions of higher learning. In order to balance the power, representative committees can promote policies or resolutions, but they need a majority vote and approval from other constituents. For example, the faculty senate could propose a new program, but the president could overturn it.

Article II of the U.S. Constitution speaks to the power of the executive branch. Section 1, in particular, dictates that "the executive Power shall be vested in a President of the United States of America." Section 3 further stipulates that "he shall from time to time give to the Congress Information of the State of the Union, and recommend to their Consideration such Measures as he shall judge necessary and expedient." At a college or university we consider the president/chancellor to be the executive who must report to the institution's constituents as a matter of fact.

Article III of the U.S. Constitution is reserved for discussion of the judicial branch. Section 1 begins with the following: "The judicial Power of the United States, shall be vested in one supreme Court, and in such inferior Courts as the Congress may from time to time ordain and establish."

This concept will be covered in much more depth in the subsequent chapters; however, for now we can consider the importance of a third power to establish a firm rule of checks and balances and to hear grievances of the constituents. Further, the judicial branch has the ability to declare any executive rule unconstitutional. While colleges may not have a governing body serving in the role as an impartial judiciary, some sort of oversight should be considered.

The first three Articles of the U.S. Constitution are reserved for the three branches of the federal government. Article IV addresses issues related to how the various states interact and their rights. Article V speaks of amendments to the Constitution. Of particular interest is the first sentence in Section 1—"The Congress, whenever two thirds of both Hoses shall deem it necessary, shall propose Amendments to the Constitution." Articles VI and VII refer to the authority of the new nation and ratification of the state constitutions.

The first ten amendments to the Constitution are known as the Bill of Rights. The First Amendment states, "Congress shall make no law respecting an establishment of religion, or prohibiting the free exercise thereof; or abridging the freedom of speech, or of the press; or of the right of the people peaceably to assemble, and to petition the Government for a redress of grievances." When employees cross the doorway at work, they should not lose their rights of free speech and assembly. And they should be able to challenge management's decisions, all without fear of retribution.

Seventeen additional amendments to the Constitution followed the original Bill of Rights. The Twelfth Amendment states, "The Electors shall meet in their respective states and vote by ballot for President and Vice-President." Simply said for the purpose of this book, faculty, staff, and students should have a say in the hiring of their executive.

The Seventeenth Amendment modifies Article I, Section 3 of the U.S. Constitution by defining the term of senators. The Twentieth Amendment further modifies Article I, Section 4 of the Constitution by defining the terms of the executive branch and requirements of assembly of Congress. Limiting the president to two terms in office was the direction of the Twenty-Second Amendment. This amendment is mentioned here only because this author strongly does not believe that a university executive should have term limits.

Now, what are the lessons we can take from these historical documents? From the Declaration of Independence we learn of the natural and inherent equality of the people and the need to treat everyone with dignity and respect. Furthermore, all governance power and authority is derived from the people—from the constituents, if you will.

From Article I of the Constitution, we learn of representative government, the need for balance of power, majority rule with the protection of rights of the minority, the need for regular public meetings of the representative bodies, the need for transparency to deliberations, the need for open records, that persons cannot serve on two governing bodies at once (principle of balance of power), and how rules and policies can be made (principle of checks and balances).

Article II of the U.S. Constitution tells us that the executive reports to the people. Article III shows us that a judicial body is needed for checks and balances and to allow for the people to air their grievances. Article V explains how amendments are to be promulgated.

The Bills of Rights and the other amendments to the U.S. Constitution have two implications for higher education governance. In the First Amendment, we learn that we must provide for freedom of speech and assembly, and that we need to create a place and procedures for the workers to challenge their officials. The Twelfth Amendment explains that the people vote for their executive.

It would seem then that democratic institutions are founded with the understanding of several key values and with a number of critical procedures, protocols, and doctrines in place in order to make these democratic values breathe. The critical attributes of any democratic institution, therefore, are:

- *Liberty:* personal freedom, free flow of information and ideas, open debate, and freedom of assembly[35]
- *Common Good:* greater benefit for all; majority rule while protecting the rights of the minority[36]
- *Justice:* fair treatment, shared decision-making[37]
- *Equality:* no class hierarch[38]
- *Diversity:* diversity and representation of both the people of opinions[39]
- *Honesty, Openness, and Fairness:* in all interactions with each other[40]

In order for these values to become alive, certain mechanisms and institutional behaviors must take place. Decision-making must be shared, transparent, and open.[41] This requires that information be shared freely with the people. The people need to be empowered. Where it is too cumbersome to be done directly, indirect empowerment must be created through representative governance.

In order to guard against any one person or group from becoming too dominant, a system of checks and balances needs to exist.[42] This leads to a separation of powers in order to limit the powers of any person or governing body.[43] Finally, a rule of law (or policies and rules) must be established to provide for fairness and equity.[44]

March and Olsen link the political ideas of democracy to our public institutions. "An institutionalized, free public sphere based on popular participation, public reasoning, criticism, and justification is supposed to guarantee truth-oriented opinion formation and the development of authentic identities."

"Public deliberations and majority voting institutionalized in representative assemblies are supposed to secure political equality in political decision-making. Bureaucratically organized agencies are supposed to assure efficient, qualified, and impartial implementation of policies."[45] Hilary Wainwright promulgated several imperative conditions in order for democratic participation to exist:

In order for participatory democracy to attain its own legitimacy . . . certain conditions need to be in place. First, if any form of participatory democracy is to achieve legitimacy as a source of power over decisions concerning the government of a locality, it needs to be open at its foundations to everyone affected by such decisions—even if only a minority participate. Openness is not just a formality. . . . Second, there need to be mutually agreed and openly negotiated rules. . . . A third condition, always difficult to preserve, is the autonomy of the participatory process from the state. . . . But these relationships depend on equality: participatory institutions need to have their own life and dynamism, and know that the elected body respects this. This egalitarianism leads to a fourth condition: the genuine sharing of knowledge. . . . The process must get results. It must not be seen as just another consultation exercise that leads nowhere.[46]

To which Cheney and his collaborators added, "Generally speaking, we characterize workplace democracy as referring to those principles and practices designed to engage and 'represent' (in the multiple senses of the term) as many relevant individuals and groups as possible in the formulation, execution, and modification of work-related activities."[47]

A variety of scholars in democratic workplaces have explicated these concepts, and it would be worthwhile to hear at least a portion of their reasoning. Liberty demands personal freedom, a free flow of information, open debate, and freedom of assembly. To this end, Cheney et al. further stipulate, "Democratization can be operationally defined in terms of the extent of genuine opportunities for dissent and discussion."[48] We must ensure that faculty, staff, and students are not punished for sharing their concerns. In fact, we must provide opportunities for people to meet and discuss these concerns and their ideas.

When it comes to supporting the common good, we find that decision-making must be based upon an equitable voting system. From their review of the literature, March and Olsen added that there are "several fundamental rights and rules necessary for a democratic process: open inquiry, discussion, enlightened understanding, equal consideration, effective participation, and a decision reached by some system of voting that respects the essential equality of the citizens."[49]

Not only must people have a say in issues that impact them, but they must be able to vote where prudent. Further, all groups need to be represented and their representatives must be chosen by the constituents.

Identification of democratic governing principles and values is critical as we begin to draw inferences to the workplace. Putting them into practice will be quite a task. Chapters 4 and 5 will develop implications for developing more truly democratic shared governance approaches across all constituent groups across our institutions of higher education.

Before we return to our journey with Vice President Sam, let us learn from the personal perspective of an experienced and current professional staff member who has been instrumental in the genesis, growth, and implementation of a staff council utilizing principles of shared governance and decision-making.

STAFF COUNCIL—KATY COKER

With roughly 150 full-time and part-time professional academic staff, this private liberal arts college had enjoyed decades of hardworking, loyal, and conscientious employees fulfilling their responsibilities. Still, like at many institutions of higher learning, they found themselves working in silos and felt underappreciated or as "second-class citizens."

Three years ago, senior administration approved the creation and development of a staff council. At that time, the VPAA began to meet with a small cadre of staff members to discuss this endeavor and how to make it happen. He served as liaison to the President's Cabinet.

This small group of academic staff were very enthusiastic and energetic to begin the spring semester. The first order of business was a meeting with the VPAA, myself, and another staff leader. We brainstormed ideas about the purpose, who else to get involved in this initial developmental phase, and how to begin the process. Before bringing in other people to this discussion, however, we decided to investigate Staff Councils at other colleges. So, we began to look at different websites and called people that we knew from other institutions.

Immediately we knew we needed to create a purpose statement, create a few critical committees, and begin deciding on membership. Ultimately, this work would lead to the creation of bylaws and elections. We needed help, so we brought in a handful of staff colleagues and shared with them our ideas and thoughts from our investigation of other institutions. The response was overwhelmingly positive.

As a small ad hoc committee we drafted a purpose statement that, for the most part, remains the same, today. A couple of committee members began drafting temporary bylaws, and others drafted committee charges and membership parameters. All of this came together fairly quickly over the early part of the spring months.

We chose to have twelve Council members from different parts of the college, including two at-large seats. The other area representatives came from (one each): Human Resources, VPAA Office, and President's Office; Athletics; Business Office, Registrar, and Financial Aid; Office of Institutional Advancement; Student Affairs; Admissions; Administrative Services; Campus Police, Information Technology; and, Academic Schools, Library.

Our goal was to put together an elections process during the fall and hold elections in the spring semester. But, in the meantime, we asked for volunteers from these groups to serve on this initial Council. We had no problem finding enthusiastic volunteers.

These volunteers created four committees: Executive, Bylaws and Elections, Staff Development, and Communications/Special Projects. The Executive Committee was made up of a chairperson, vice chairperson, secretary/treasurer, and eventually to include past chair. It should be noted that the administration provided us a $5,000 budget for our first year.

Kickoff

For a moment, I would like to explain some context for our official kickoff. Our college has an annual Welcome Back Week tradition for all faculty members at the beginning of August. A wide variety of events and meetings take place throughout the week for the faculty members.

This week culminated with a big event gathering all faculty and senior administration together as an assembly. This day starts off with a breakfast, followed by the president, vice presidents, and faculty senate chair giving opening day remarks—a state of the college, so to speak. Lunch follows, and then all faculty attend a variety of workshops and professional development activities throughout the afternoon.

In the past, no such events or activities had taken place for academic staff. Nor, did staff even attend the opening breakfast, opening session, or lunch. Rather, staff members worked in their offices like any other day. Truly, there was a culture of an academic community and a staff community. The Staff Council changed all this.

While we were working on bylaws and membership/election issues, we had a major and pressing endeavor. We wanted to kickoff the Staff Council during Opening Day. Our senior administration, along with the faculty senate chair, agreed to have all staff attend Opening Day activities (breakfast, opening assembly, lunch, and afternoon sessions). Rather than the traditional Faculty Assembly, it would be referred to as Community Assembly.

This meant we would need to unveil a: purpose statement; a description of committees and activities; and, membership. We also knew that faculty workshops in the afternoon would not be relatable to our work, so we needed to create workshops that pertained to us. The summer proved to be busy.

Our preparations for Opening Day proved to be a huge success. The auditorium was filled with an equal mix of faculty and staff for the opening session. After the president and vice presidents presented their opening remarks, the focus shifted to a brief presentation by the faculty senate chair, followed by a brief presentation from one of our staff leaders who explained the purpose of our newly forming Staff Council and a description of the afternoon activities. As our college had a theme of "student success," the morning session concluded with a presentation by a committee of faculty and staff discussing plans to support student success in the upcoming year.

Faculty and staff then ate lunch together in the Student Commons. Following our common meal, the faculty headed to one of the academic buildings for a large assembly followed by a number of mandatory sessions in breakout rooms. Staff exited to another academic building for a full assembly followed by breakout sessions. The breakout sessions focused on: Owning Student Success (the theme for faculty, as well); Center for Teaching & Learning/ Staff Development; What do you expect from your Staff Council?; Best Practices; and, Student Employment (process and software).

Our staff assembly served as an opportunity for our ad hoc committee to describe in greater detail our purpose, ideas for structure and membership, and focus for the upcoming year. We were met with great enthusiasm and took plenty of time to answer questions. Then, we broke into smaller sessions as described above.

These smaller sessions were each chaired by ad hoc committee members and notes were recorded. Each session was concluded with a paper survey provided to each attendee in which they were asked what they were looking for from a staff council.

Moving Forward

Prior to the creation of the Staff Council, staff members had no or little formal role in decision-making processes. Their advice or recommendations were sought out only in an informal or ad hoc fashion. As a collective body, there was no formal recognition of professional staff members; morale was low. This began to change in the following years as the institution transitioned to formal recognition and structures for the Staff Council.

The major issues that emerged from staff surveys included: Communication/Special Projects, Staff Development, Staff Recognition, and Employee Health & Wellness. As such, committees were created for each of these areas, even without formal staff council membership. We had work to do, and we were going to capitalize on our energy and momentum. At the same time, we continued to work on bylaws development, and elections for council membership.

The Communications/Special Projects Committee created a portal page. This site highlights our purpose statement, bylaws, and Council member notes. All Staff Council agendas, minutes, and events are archived, as well. During the first year, this committee also created a monthly electronic newsletter sent to all employees.

Earlier, the VPAA created a Center for Teaching and Learning (CTL). Under the umbrella of this center was housed professional development activities for both faculty and professional staff members. The VPAA provided the CTL a budget of $10,000. The Staff Development Committee provided support for both individual and group professional development initiatives from this office. The CTL was also responsible for instructional technology and the college's Quality Enhancement Plan (QEP) which supported student success initiatives.

The Staff Recognition Committee immediately created an Employee of the Month Award. Nominations are made through an electronic form and winners are identified by the committee members. The staff newsletter announces the winners each month and they receive small gift awards.

The Employee Health & Wellness Committee was created after a great number of requests from staff indicating such initiatives in the August survey. The recurring team Step Challenge was the first activity we created.

Winners are announced in the staff council newsletter and they receive a small reward.

In our second full year of the staff council we found ourselves in a bit of a sophomore slump. We continued with all of our initiatives of the first year, and our sense of purpose and direction remained focused and high. But, with our busy schedules, including intensive involvement in the college's new strategic planning initiatives, attendance at council meetings dwindled somewhat.

We have added other initiatives later in our first and second year, however. We have held two social events for all employees on the academic quad and a tailgate party for a lacrosse game. Each month we have a reduced lunch day for employees in the commons, and we have initiated a new summer-hours program for staff. We also took it upon ourselves to examine a workflow process for students from the time they applied to the time they became alumni to see how we could be more efficient and customer-friendly.

The Future

Our creation and development of a staff council has been even more successful and rewarding than we had hoped. It has been a wonderful endeavor that has taken a tremendous amount of effort and support across the campus. Morale has improved dramatically. We now have formal roles in strategic planning initiatives. Administration often seeks staff membership on both ad hoc and standing committees as a matter of course. We are responsible for our own professional development and have the support of our administration.

In the coming years, we plan to play a bigger role in our annual Welcome Back Week and recreate the initial excitement of the staff council we had our first year. We also need to rotate some original council members off and add new members as stated in our bylaws. This should help us bring new excitement, energy, and ideas.

When it comes to the democratic principles espoused in this book, we do see more transparency in decision-making. We do have representation and involvement, and communication is stronger than ever. There is still work to do, though. We need to wrestle with our roles in shared governance as depicted in table 4.6: The Pillars Responsibility Matrix. We can say, though, that we are confident and that we are up to the challenge.

SAM—EVERYBODY'S WORKING FOR THE WEEKEND

Sam was grateful for the weekend. Her younger sister Leslie, the president and CEO of a moderate-sized home healthcare business, was visiting for a couple of days. Leslie was in the area as she was taking two days to interview candidates for director positions of two new facilities.

The two sisters had always been best friends, albeit with a common streak of competitive nature. They spent early Saturday morning hiking the scenic lake route at Vista State Park. Sam often hiked here early in the morning and was dying to show Leslie. They had a picnic lunch in the shade of a juniper grove and chatted about the challenges of work, memories of fun childhood day-trips with their parents, and hopes for the future. Since neither had time to prepare a lunch, they stopped off at the deli, that Sam was becoming all too familiar with, and bought sushi rolls, coleslaw, bean chips, and bottled water.

Sam talked of her concerns with possible budget cuts, trying to innovate some new ideas, but it was mostly about how she was struggling with a culture of homeostasis. Leslie, on the other hand, wanted to find new, young managers who were innovative and energetic but had the experience, maturity, and loyalty of her generation. Sam felt Leslie needed to spend more time on college campuses to get to know the new generation of future leaders and to start hiring more interns. Leslie, on the other hand, felt that Sam and her professors needed to spend some more time in the real world. They both agreed with one another.

After their lunch, they raced back to campus to watch the Founders University football Eagles host their conference rivals—the Jepson Jackrabbits. Both teams were undefeated, and the winner would likely take the division title to the conference championship. Sam and Leslie sat up high in the box seats reserved for dignitaries and the like. It was a hot and sunny afternoon with not a cloud in the sky. The score was tied 7–7 at halftime as the sisters watched the Founders marching band perform. This band could stand toe to toe with any band in the region. Some people said that more people came to watch the band than watch the game. Indeed, the band had a swagger, a ton of energy, and the drum core was second to none.

Athletic director Dirk Zentkowski had spent the second quarter sitting with the sisters and sharing his insights, even when none were asked for. During one timeout, however, Dirk caught Sam off guard. He began, "Sam, I've thought a lot about your idea of starting a staff council. Two things come to my mind. If you do start a council, please don't forget the Athletic Department. Too often we are left out of things like this."

Sam gave a nod of knowing approval. "That makes a lot of sense, Dirk. I promise Athletics will be involved. What's the other thing you have in mind?"

Eagerly, Dirk continued. "Don't stop with a Staff Council. Let's reinvigorate the Student Government Association. They seem like an organization in name only. It's just a resume-builder for these kids. They really don't do anything other than organize events. They could do so much more!"

Quietly Sam agreed only nodding her head. She had multiple thoughts. "I wasn't planning on getting involved in student government, but such an effort would be appropriate." And, "I hate it when people call our students, 'kids.' These students are 19–23 years old. If they weren't in college they would likely have jobs and live in apartments. They would be adults. We have to stop treating them and talking about them as kids. That would change our interactions with them and our expectations of them, and maybe ourselves."

Then Dirk made an offer the sisters felt they could not refuse when he asked, "Would you guys like to join me on the sidelines for the second half? The game is a lot different down there than it is up here. Seriously, come join me; it'll be fun."

Sam and Leslie jumped at the opportunity. As they walked out onto the field, they immediately felt a very different sense of energy. They turned to the stands and saw the crowd enjoying themselves, singing and chanting, and everyone having a great time. Then, the two teams came running back onto the field. The crowd stood up with even more energy, and the players looked a lot bigger and actually kind of frightening. There were ripped jerseys and numbers, blackened rubber stains on pants from the artificial turf, frayed tape on fingers and wrists, several blood spattered uniforms, and lots and lots of sweat.

The energy seemed different than before the game. It wasn't really excitement; it was more of a strident focus and really some anger. Plenty of shouting at one another with a few curse words thrown in for affect. Nearby, two players chest bumped each other sending them backward and bumping into Sam. She didn't know who was more startled, she or he. In any case, Sam was taken aback when an assistant coach grabbed one player by the face mask and growled, "If you don't punch someone in the mouth, I'm gonna kick you in the ass and put a freshmen in for you!" The player, who had a bloodied rug burn over his entire elbow ran onto the field as the referee blew the whistle for the kickoff. The P.A. system blared some loud music which was unfamiliar to Sam. The energy level had gone back up dramatically, and both women had lumps in their throats.

Sam couldn't take her eyes off the player whom she just witnessed getting humiliated by the coach. As the ball was kicked, he sprinted full speed along with his teammates. You could hear the thumping of their feet and the rattling of their pads as they sprinted down in unison. Then utter chaos ensued. The Jepson player caught the ball and sprinted about ten yards straight upfield and turned on a dime and headed straight toward the sideline where Leslie and Sam watched.

Number 97, the player Sam was watching turned in the direction of the runner. As he turned, he got nailed by a Jackrabbit—number 53. Number 53 hit 97 in the side of his helmet. The sound of the impact was startling, followed by a groan Sam had never heard before. Number 97 flipped from his feet and landed sprawled out on his side managing to trip up the runner.

The Jackrabbit players screamed and high-fived number 53 for his hit and ran off the field celebrating. Number 97 stayed on the ground for just a couple of seconds but got up and shook his head before heading to the sideline. The same coach came up and slapped him on the pants and growled, "Now, that's what I'm talking about. Next time don't fall down!" Sam was wide-eyed at this whole scene. Should she tell President Davis on Monday? She looked at the player; she just saw a vacant look in his eyes.

The whistle blew and numerous players were sent running on and off the field, again in unison and they got into a huddle. More and more events like this took place over the afternoon. Great coordination punctuated with moments of chaos and apparent disorder, all coming back to order again. Eventually, the game finished. Founders won 24–10. The crowd was ecstatic, and the players were totally exhausted, very happy, and walked off the field. Some players who never got in the game had plenty of energy and playfully pushed each other around.

Sam's mind ran rapidly about the games' events. What lessons did she learn? How did she feel about some of what she witnessed? Could she take away any lessons from all of this? And what did Leslie think about all this?

The sisters went home to clean up. Sam sat down at her computer to check her email while Leslie left to meet a prospective candidate for an interview. Leslie felt Sam has a great job where she can have fun watching football games on Saturdays. Sam felt it was a bit odd that Leslie conducted an interview on a weekend.

While Leslie was meeting with a prospective manager, Sam read an email from Professor Sinclair. He sent a very brief note to her asking how she was doing in her preparations for her speaking engagement with his U.S. History class. "Oh my gosh!" Leslie said out loud to herself. "I totally forgot. I have to speak on Wednesday morning."

Sam spent the next two hours putting together an outline. She was still haunted by Dr. Sinclair's earlier discussion where he told her not to make it too didactic but engaging. She knew she needed to explain the organizational structure of the three pillars of shared governance and their responsibilities. But, she wasn't really sure precisely what those responsibilities were, just vague ideas. She decided to look in the faculty handbook and bylaws first thing Monday morning.

Sam also thought about general principles of democracy and how they might be pertinent. Checks and balances, coequal branches, transparency, majority rule, protection of the minority, and freedom of speech and assembly. That seemed like a good start. But, as she began to think more on it, some of these didn't make sense. Maybe a political democracy wasn't a good fit for democratic decision-making in higher education. Shared governance was a better phrase than democratic governance.

For example, are the three pillars in higher education really coequal branches? Certainly not. The board has ultimate authority, and the president and his executive cabinet are the bosses. So, that didn't work cleanly. Majority rule? No. The faculty were the majority, and if the majority rule was true, then the faculty would get their way. Not only that, there were at least as many staff as faculty, and they have no voice. And, what about all the students? Students outnumbered all faculty and staff combined.

And again, how to make this presentation engaging? Sam was struggling. She struggled. She struggled some more. She was engaged, that's for sure. Then it struck her. "I'm engaged. I'm engaged with this struggle! Just like Paulo Freire said, 'Don't take away the dignity of their struggle.' That's it! I'm going to let the students jump into this struggle with me. We're going to argue together. We're going to be congruent in our approach to learning this topic as the principles of the topic demand. In other words, we're going to voice our ideas in a free exchange. We're going to debate and learn from one another." Sam was excited about her brilliant idea and self-dialogue.

With that, Leslie let herself back in after her dinner/interview out. She really didn't look too pleased. Apparently the interview didn't go too well. Leslie felt the young man was bright and interesting. She just wasn't sure he was ready for the job. Could he run the agency? Could he be a boss?

The sisters talked for a while about their hike and then the football game. Sam remarked how different the game is on the field than from on TV or up in the stands. Leslie, on the other hand, thought there were comparisons to work.

"Didn't all seem just so chaotic? I mean, I know a little bit about football, but it's just a whirlwind of activity that doesn't all seem to make sense. But, then it all comes back together in total unison before falling into utter chaos and back into order."

Sam jumped in. "I know what you mean. I once heard a professor use the term, 'chaortic.' There's always an underlying order in what might appear as disorder or chaos. When you simply see a snapshot, it looks like chaos. But, if you look at the entirety of the event over time and space you see the order. But, in this case, it surely is violent."

Leslie laughed, "Yeah, chaortic. Kinda reminds me of your strategic planning. Always appears in disarray, but maybe there really is order."

This flippant response actually gave Sam pause. Perhaps Leslie was onto something. Maybe part of her job was to help people keep the focus and remember the original themes and vision of the planning—to see the order in the chaos of their everyday hectic schedules. But, that's too much thinking for now.

Leslie and Sam decided to wind down by watching a movie suggested by one of Leslie's coworkers: Twelve Angry Men. She had an old black-and-white DVD of the version with Henry Fonda and Jack Klugman. As it turned out, this movie would have a profound impact on Sam for years to come.

These two sisters first saw the movie when they were in high school. They were both enamored with Henry Fonda—such a handsome man with a caring heart. His character stood up against eleven other jurors convinced of the guilt of a young immigrant boy. Decades ago they watched the movie with eyes toward entertainment and teenage rebellion against society. Tonight, they watched the movie through lenses of life experiences, work responsibilities, and by wearing the shoes of mature adults. This movie seemed different than the one of years ago.

Sam was struck at the perseverance of Henry Fonda's character. While he wasn't sure of the boy's innocence or guilt, he was sure of and dedicated to the process of discovery. She was also amazed at how he, for the most part, kept calm and didn't demean others. Leslie was struck that he kept to his values and kept seeking the answers over and over again. He was relentless and made certain everyone's voice was heard. He wouldn't move forward without these conditions being met.

All of this reminded Leslie of the movie, Lincoln, starring Daniel Day-Lewis. This film did an exceptional job of capturing President Abraham Lincoln's inner turmoils of the myriad conflicts during the Civil War and his dedication to the abolishment of slavery.

Leslie marveled, "He actually surrounded himself with people on his own cabinet who strongly disagreed with him. As a matter of fact, they thought he wasn't intelligent and was backwards in experience. They fought him every step of the way, yet he was dogged in his perseverance."

"You know what struck me about Lincoln, Leslie," added Sam, "He was disarming, colloquial, and told stories. He really understood the people of the country, and he tried to understand those who fought him."

"And it killed him. . ." Leslie concluded, "Lincoln was our nation's greatest leader. He was transformational, but he was also transitional. He never got to see the fruits of his labor."

Both Leslie and Sam sat there, quietly. After what seemed like forever, Sam said, "But he changed the world." She paused. "Talk about change. I have another movie, The Efficiency Expert starring Anthony Hopkins as the protagonist and a very young Russell Crowe as a nasty antagonist." The two sisters were binge watching the oldies, tonight.

Sam absolutely loved this movie. Leslie was somewhat ambivalent. At least Leslie thought it was funny to see these actors when they were so much younger in a rather lighthearted affair. Sam, on the other hand, saw this poignant film in terms of its development of the lead character in his change from the stoic by-the-book bureaucrat to an embedded leader of a working community. In any case, it was a fun way to end a busy day. It was a good day for the sisters to be together again.

NOTES

1. Fritjof Capra, *The Hidden Connections: A Science of Sustainable Living* (New York: Anchor Books, 2004), 34.

2. Charles Heckscher, "Defining the Post-Bureaucratic Type," In Charles Heckscher and Anne Donnellon, eds, *The Post-Bureaucratic Organization: New Perspectives on Organizational Change* (Thousand Oaks, CA: Sage, 1994), 24.

3. Charles Heckscher, R. Eisenstat, and T. Rice, "Transformational Processes," In Charles Heckscher and Lynda Applegate, eds, *The Post-Bureaucratic Organization: New Perspectives on Organizational Change* (Thousand Oaks, CA: Sage, 1994), 147.

4. Capra, *The Hidden Connections*, 103.

5. Richard Wells and J. Stevens Picou, "The Becoming Place: A Study of Educational Change in a Small College," *Research in Higher Education* 17 (1) (1982), 28.

6. Wells and Picou, "The Becoming Place," 29.

7. Francis Neumann Jr., "Organizational Structures to Match the New Information-Rich Environments: Lessons from the Study of Chaos," *Public Productivity and Management Review* (September 1997), 95.

8. James March and Johan Olsen, *Democratic Governance* (New York: The Free Press, 1995).

9. March and Olsen, *Democratic Governance*, 192.

10. Edward Greenberg, *Workplace Democracy: The Political Effects of Participation* (Ithaca, NY: Cornell University Press, 1986), 28. For the most insightful and exhaustive review of the loss of democracy in the workplace the reader is invited to examine Howard Zinn's book, *Declarations of Independence: Cross-Examining American Ideology* (New York: Harper Collins, 1990).

11. George Cheney et al., "Democracy, Participation, and Communication at Work: A Multidisciplinary Review," *Communication Yearbook* 21 (2004), 54.

12. Zelda Gamson and Henry Levin, "Obstacles to the Survival of Democratic Organizations," In Robert Jackal and Henry M. Levin, eds. *Worker Cooperatives in America* (Berkeley, CA: University of California Press, 1984), 223.

13. William Halal, *The New Management: Bringing Democracy and Markets Inside Organizations* (San Francisco: Berrett-Koehler, 1998), 93.

14. Peter Bachrach and Aryeh Botwinick, *Power and Empowerment: A Radical Theory of Participatory Democracy* (Philadelphia: Temple University Press, 1992), 103.

15. Adrianna Kezar and Elizabeth Holcombe, "Shared Leadership in Higher Education: Important Lessons from Research and Practice," *American Council on Education* 29 (2017), 18.

16. John Smyth, "The Socially Just Alternative to the 'Self-Managing School'" In Keith Leithwood et al. eds. *International Handbook of Educational Leadership and Administration* (The Netherlands: Kluwer Academic Publishers, 1996), 1097. Smyth also explained that governing bodies maintain priority setting and leave the detail work for the teachers and call it empowerment. Furthermore, requisite resources for sites to carry out their decisions are seriously limited, giving them little practical power.

17. Zinn, *Declarations of Independence*, 219.

18. Paulo Freire, *Pedagogy of the Oppressed* (New York: Continuum, 1970), 45.

19. Maxim Voronov and Peter T. Coleman, "Beyond the Ivory Towers: Organizational Power Practices and a 'Practical' Critical Postmodernism," *The Journal of Applied Behavioral Science,* 39 (2) (June 2003), 173.

20. Fareed Zakaria, *The Future of Freedom: Illiberal Democracy at Home and Abroad* (New York: W. W. Norton & Company, 2003), 102. Drawing similar conclusions to the workplace, Gordon stipulated, "Some social theorists . . . have observed that groups, even devoutly democratic ones, seem to evolve into an oligarchical structure, with power relinquished by the majority to a small handful of 'leaders.'" Frederick Gordon, "Bureaucracy: Can We do Better? Can We do Worse?" In Heckscher and Applegate, 215.

21. Voronov and Coleman, "Beyond the Ivory Towers," 176.

22. Samuel Huntington, *The Clash of Civilizations: Remaking of World Order* (New York: Simon & Schuster, 1997), 71.

23. Bachrach and Botwinick, *Power and Empowerment*, 164.

24. Teresa Harrison, "Designing the Post-Bureaucratic Organization: Toward Egalitarian Organizational Structure," *Australian Journal of Communication* 19 (2) (1992), 20.

25. Smyth, "The Socially Just Alternative to the 'Self-Managing School,'" 1097.

26. Gamson and Levin, "Obstacles to the Survival of Democratic Organizations," 223.

27. Greenberg, *Workplace Democracy*, 132.

28. Peter Block, *Stewardship: Choosing Service over Self-Interest* (San Francisco: Berrett-Koehler, 1996), 238.

29. Greenberg, *Workplace Democracy*, 170.

30. www.constitutioncenter.org.

31. Some readers may feel that these fundamental constitutional values were taken out of context in their application to the workplace. The reader is invited to read the full document as cited in the endnotes following this chapter.

32. The discussion of core values of the American Constitution and Constitutional Principles were taken from CIVITAS: *A Frame Work for Civic Education*, a collaborative project of the Center for Civic Education and the Council for the Advancement of Citizenship, National Council for the Social Studies Bulletin, No. 86, 1991. Borrowed from www.constitutioncenter.org/explore/TheUS.Constitution/index.shmtl. The core values are cited from page 1 and the constitutional principles from page 2. For additional insights into the principles of democracy, the reader is invited to visit https://web.standford.edu/~ldiamond/iraq/DemocracyEducation0204.htm by Larry

Diamond. The reader is also invited to visit the website of the Library of Congress at www.loc.gov/law/help/guide/federal/usconst.php.

33. Huntington, *The Clash of Civilizations*, 110.

34. Zakaria, *The Future of Freedom*, 157.

35. March and Olsen, *Democratic Governance*, 22.

36. Greenberg, *Workplace Democracy*, 170.

37. D. Dotlich and P. Cairo, *Unnatural Leadership: Going Against Intuition and Experience to Develop Ten New Leaderships Instincts* (San Francisco: Jossey-Bass, 2002), 162. "Empowerment in complex organizations, however, is essential; it's impossible to compete and grow if the people who are furthest from the customers are making the decisions. Leaders need to trust that those on the front line are in the best position to make decisions." To which Atkinson added, "The management principles of democracy, profit-sharing, and information require a collegial approach to sharing information and decision-making. The conventional top-down flows of information, decision-making authority, and responsibility give way to an environment where the opinion of the *knowledge worker* [emphasis in original] is valued, sought out, and considered." Anthony Atkinson, "The Promise of Employee Involvement," *CMA Magazine* 3, (April 1990), 8.

38. Bachrach and Botwinick, *Power and Empowerment*, 41.

39. Democracies require diversity of people participating and sharing their opinions, and democratic organizations need flexibility in operationalizing their values. But "participation is not equivalent to democracy," E. Davis and Russel Lansbury, *Democracy and Control in the Workplace* (Melbourne, Australia: Longman Cheshire, 1986), 35. "Democracy thrives on instruments for creating and maintaining diversity. It profits from public criticism and debate, from conflict over values and rules, and from differences that lead to experimentation with alternative practices and exploration of new visions." March and Olsen, *Democratic Governance*, 169.

40. Zinn, *Declarations of Independence*, 211–212.

41. March and Olsen, *Democratic Governance*, 150–152.

42. CIVITAS: *A Frame Work for Civic Education*.

43. Ibid.

44. March and Olsen, *Democratic Governance*, 126.

45. Ibid., 224.

46. Hilary Wainwright, *Reclaim the State: Experiments in Popular Democracy* (London: Verso, 2003), 188–189.

47. Cheney et al., "Democracy, Participation, and Communication at Work," 40.

48. Ibid., 61.

49. March and Olsen, *Democratic Governance*, 22.

Chapter 4

Here's How

Man's capacity for justice makes democracy possible, but man's inclination to injustice makes democracy necessary.[1]

Reinhold Niebuhr

After a tremendous amount of debate during the Philadelphia Convention, the American founding fathers drafted a constitution to be ratified by the states. Their struggles focused on such issues as the balance of power, a system of checks and balances, and even the number of branches in the government.

The role of the executive received a great deal of scrutiny. In the end, our three "branches" (executive, legislative, and judicial) were agreed upon (see table 4.1). Obviously, this was a political tripartite model. In the Industrial Age, the business world embraced a corporate model (see table 4.2) that was operationally very different than the political model.

K–12 school systems adopted their own parallel model; Patrick Dolan referred to these three branches as "anchors" (superintendent, union, and board—as depicted in Table 4.3).[2]

This model presented by Patrick Dolan suggests the three leadership pillars (anchors) represent in K–12 schools—the board of education, the superintendent, and the teachers union. Within the pyramid are various central office administrative units, and at the bottom of the pyramid are sub-pyramids representing individual schools with principals at the top, teachers and staff in the middle, and students at the bottom. Parents and community members are represented by an arc outside of the pyramid. (This graphic is described in figure 5.1).

Traditional higher education, shared governance models also have three anchors of authority: the board of trustees, the president, and the faculty

Table 4.1 Democratic (Political) Governance Model

Democratic Governance Model		
Legislative	*Executive*	*Judicial*
Senate & House of Representatives	President	Supreme Court
*Creates the Laws	*Executes the Laws	*Interprets the Laws

senate. At the bottom of the university pyramid would be individual college pyramids with deans on the top and faculty, staff, and students at the bottom. Like the K–12 model, the students and staff really don't have representation in the conventional model.

If we were to examine the political democratic governance and corporate governance models, we would see that each has three primary authority groups, but their foci are dissimilar. The democratic governance model relies on three coequal branches, while the corporate governance model clearly does not follow equal power across the branches. Likewise, traditional higher education governance models and K–12 schools models are not based on a coequal balance. Their intent is more about sharing in the process of decision-making.

With all its inherent foibles, the democratic governance model does equalize the balance of power among all three branches and provides for a system of checks and balances so that one branch does not overreach its authority. The U.S. Constitution enumerates the checks on all three branches. As particularly germane to the focus of this book, the legislative branch checks the executive branch with the ability to override presidential vetoes. The legislative branch checks the judicial branch by approving federal judges, and it has the ability to create constitutional amendments.

As the legislative branch is a bicameral body, it also checks itself, since both houses must pass bills, and these houses also initiate budgetary bills. The executive branch checks the legislative branch with its own veto authority, the vice president is the president of the Senate, and it can call Congress into an emergency session. It checks the judicial branch with the ability to appoint judges and with the authority to pardon.

The executive branch has a self-regulating check by allowing the vice president and cabinet to rule that the president is unfit to carry out his or her duties. Finally, the judicial branch checks both the executive and legislative

Table 4.2 Corporate Governance Model

Corporate Governance Model		
Board of Trustees	Administration/CEO	Union/Worker
*Sets the Vision	*Executes the Vision	*Protects Employee Rights

Table 4.3   K–12 School Governance Model

School Board	Superintendent	Unions
*Sets Vision/Policies	*Executes Vision/Policies	*Ensures anchors Operate within their scope of authority

Source: Patrick Dolan. 1994. *Restructuring our Schools: A Primer on Systemic Change*. Kansas City, MO: Systems and Organizations, 17.

branches via the process of judicial review in order to make certain that neither branch is operating outside its scope of responsibilities.[3]

The corporate governance model does not balance the power, nor does it necessarily provide for a satisfactory system of checks and balances to counter the power in each anchor. The board of directors set the vision and priorities; the CEO executes the vision and priorities; and the union protects the employees' rights. At best, this model checks itself through adversarial relationships—each anchor needs the other in order to exist in a quasi-symbiotic coexistence.

Finally, and most troubling, the corporate governance model has the fundamental assumption that those at the top of the pyramid or hierarchy know more than those further down—those doing the work. This assumption may or may not be correct in the corporate model, but it is erroneous in professional organizations, such as those who hire doctors and professors. A different model is needed for those type of organizations, and the higher educational governance model was designed for those professionals.

The corporate model of governance is certainly not a clean fit for the culture and aims of higher education. "In the corporate model, faculty members are treated as 'employees' to be assigned to duties defined by management, rather than as largely autonomous professionals working in a college setting."[4] This puts the president of a college in a bind.

According to Birnbaum and Eckel, "In a business firm, the president or CEO is solely accountable to a board of directors. In higher education, the president functions between two layers of organizational operations—the trustees and the faculty—and is accountable to both."[5]

The difference between corporate and higher educational governance models has as much to do about purpose as it does with culture. "Unlike corporations, where there is generally one bottom line, universities have multiple bottom lines. The academic president's role is different from that of the corporate chief because of the former's commitment to a mission and a heritage. The corporate chief's obligation is to the bottom line and to shareholders' financial interests."[6]

Colleges and universities, however, have established a model of shared governance that had served them reasonably well for many decades (see table 4.4). It is the contention of this book, however, that time has slowly eroded

Table 4.4   Higher Education Shared Governance Model

Higher Education Shared Governance Model		
Board of Trustees	*President/Chancellor*	*Faculty Senate*
*Sets the Vision	*Executes the Vision	*Ensures Faculty Rights

or blurred the lines between these tripartite bodies, and our current models reflect more of a corporate model, in reality. This demands a reexamination—through our founding democratic principles and values—which will allow us to create a more robust, contemporary, and effective shared governance models for our institutions of higher education.

It is this very notion of shared governance that we have allowed to slip away very quietly and almost without notice over the years. Peter Block warned, "There is an unmistakable contradiction between the democratic values of freedom and independence and the colonial and patriarchal strategies used to manage our organizations."[7] "Central to such freedom is the right of a faculty member, without fear of reprisal or loss of influence, to criticize the administration and the governing board on matters of faculty concern. Thus the nexus between governance and academic freedom is vital."[8]

Further, the notion of "shared" causes angst and confusion to many practitioners and observers. Gary Olson attempted to clarify. "'Shared' means that everyone has a role. . . . 'Shared' doesn't mean that every constituency gets to participate at every stage. Nor does it mean that any constituency exercises complete control over the process." Olson sums it up this way:

> Clearly, when it comes to university governance, "shared" is a much more capacious concept than most people suspect. True shared governance attempts to balance maximum participation in decision making with clear accountability. That is a difficult balance to maintain. . . . Genuine shared governance gives voice (but not necessarily ultimate authority) to concerns common to all constituencies as well as to issues unique to specific groups.[9]

In the conventional model, colleges and universities have an executive embodied in a president or chancellor. It also has a board of trustees or board of regents. However, its third branch is of particular interest here. The faculty senate houses the shared governance rights of the faculty. Some campuses will further these rights to other personnel via a staff senate or council. In any case, the faculty senate provides that vehicle for professors to be engaged in decision-making pertinent to their professional domain.

Bowen and Tobin have written extensively on the governance model of higher education. It is appropriate to spend a few moments discussing the roles and responsibilities of these three governing groups at American colleges and universities. Bowen and Tobin remind us of the "traditional rights and responsibilities in the familiar areas of composition of faculty, curriculum, admissions, student life, and academic freedom."[10]

They go on to discuss the AAUP position on roles and responsibilities: "Throughout its hundred-year history, the AAUP has consistently acknowledged that governing boards and administrations have primary authority over matters affecting institutions' mission, planning, financial resources, and budgeting. By the late 1960s, however, the AAUP had begun to assert the faculty's *consultative* [emphasis added] rights in all matters affecting college and university decision making."[11]

In referencing Princeton University's shared governance policy, Bowen and Tobin explain, "The *Statement of Delegation* distinguishes among matters where the trustees exercise only 'general review' (e.g., faculty appointment processes, curricular decisions, and other academic matters), matters where trustees exercise 'prior review' (when there is a claim on funds, including the setting of budgets), and matters where there is 'authority directly exercised' by the trustees (investments, real estate transactions, and so on)."[12]

Therefore, it is the trustees' and the administrations' roles to establish vision, do strategic planning, and make broad fiscal and budgetary decisions, while faculty should have consultative roles in these areas. On the other hand, college faculty has primary responsibility in faculty hiring/promotion/tenure, curriculum, admissions standards, student life, and academic freedom. Of course, administration is critically involved in each of these areas in our contemporary institutions.

DEMOCRATIC PRINCIPLES APPLIED
TO SHARED GOVERNANCE

Now, for a moment, let's consider the core democratic values and constitutional principles discussed in chapter 3. There are five core democratic values: liberty, common good, justice, equality, and diversity. There are four constitutional principles: rule of law, separation of powers, representative government, and checks and balances.

How these core democratic values and constitutional principles are actualized in these different governance models will also be different. Eminent scholar of higher education, Clark Kerr, noted, "Academic governance in the United States has at least four features that distinguish it from patterns elsewhere."[13] These have to do with fact that college boards have little academic expertise; the preeminence of the role of the president; the nature of the structure of the institution; and, the extent of external forces involvement.

The four constitutional principles are conceptually met through the three governance pillars: executive (president), board of trustees, and faculty senate. The principle *of the rule of law* mostly comes down to formal policies and bylaws; nobody is held to standards outside expectations as formally established.

The principles of *checks and balances* and *separation of power* are most notably met through responsibilities associated with the respective pillars. In 2017, The Association of Governing Boards noted, "Boards working with key administrators and faculty leaders, hold responsibility for ensuring that the practice of shared governance embodies and advances institutional values."[14]

But, three years earlier, AGB explained, "Effective leadership requires clear lines of responsibility, good communication, and a shared commitment to the mission and long-term health of the institution by the board, the president, and the faculty. Integral leaderships reflects this vision of working together."[15]

The principle of *representative government* is met through the faculty senate, and possibly staff councils, and student government associations. Clark Kerr explained, "The university is also, to some degree, a democracy. Decisions are made that require the consent of the governed; rules are issued; and discipline exercised."[16]

But, to be clear, representational democracy should not infer that every person or group votes on every topic. In the words of Olson, "'Shared' means that everyone has a role. . . . 'Shared' doesn't mean that every constituency gets to participate at every stage. Nor does it mean that any constituency exercises complete control over the process. . . . The various stakeholders participate in well-defined parts of the process."[17]

Even more clearly, Olson notes: "True shared governance attempts to balance maximum participation in decision making with clear accountability. . . . Genuine shared governance gives voice (but not necessarily ultimate authority) to concerns common to all constituencies as well as to issues unique to specific groups."[18]

Invariably, there will be an inherent tension among the pillars as there are with any shared governance model. "As tensions continue to grow over free speech and shared governance, faculty input on core university issues will be crucial, according to Peter Bonilla, FIRE's vice president of programs. But the balance of power between a university's leaders and its constituents—and how faculty governance fits into this—still needs to be struck."[19]

Robert Scott explains the nuanced choreography necessary for the three pillars to function successfully in higher education. "As the board guides an institution through the governance, process, faculty must give their consent as the governed, while the president must lead with a mixture of authority, power, and persuasions within the context of the mandate given to the positions."[20]

Olson added, "Shared governance . . . is a delicate balance between faculty and staff participation in planning and decision-making processes, on the one hand, and administrative accountability on the other."[21] In the same breath Olson went on to stipulate, though, "The truth is that all legal authority in any university originates from one place and one place only: its governing board."

With that said, Olson reminded us, "University governance is a collaborative venture. 'Shared' governance has come to connote two complementary and sometimes overlapping concepts: giving various groups of people a share in decision-making processes, often through elected representation; and allowing certain groups to exercise primary responsibility for specific areas of decision-making."[22]

Now, with all that said, we have come to understand shared governance with three pillars. Or, as Mitchell and King have suggested, "Collegiate governance is always presented as a three-legged stool: administration, faculty, and board of trustees. The administration manages the college. The faculty has responsibility for the academic program. The trustees are the fiduciary stewards, who approve policy, and hire, nurture, and replace the president. The institutional buck generally stops with the trustees—and therein lies the problem."[23]

Rick Seltzer added to this discussion with an interview of Mitchell and quoted him as saying, "There should be a clear delineation of authority and a clear understanding—and a transparent understanding—of how power is executed on a college campus. Until then, we have a kind of mom-and-pop approach to governance, and that's not serving anyone well."[24]

The following pages will describe in detail the roles, expectations, and parameters of each of these governance groups.

The board of trustees, or in some case the board of regents, "has ultimate authority, [however] it explicitly delegates powers to the president as chief executive officer and to the faculty as guardians of academic programs and standards."[25] (The reader is invited to read the corresponding end note to this chapter detailing three types of boards in ascending strength and effectiveness.)

While the president or chancellor works closely with the board of trustees, their role remains distinctive. "Rather than serving as a corporate-style CEO, the president should serve as the chief education officer, reminding students, faculty, staff, and alumni about the institution's heritage and purpose and leading the mandate from the board to fulfill agreed-upon strategies to achiever agreed-upon goals."[26]

Boards of trustees have several primary responsibilities. "The shared governance process, through which trustees make decisions based on input from the president and faculty, takes place largely in committees."[27] Each pillar has distinctive roles and responsibilities; well-functioning boards understand their own roles and responsibilities, as well as those of the other pillars. "While shared governance fails for many reasons, the most likely cause is one group's overstepping its boundaries."[28]

With regard to responsibilities relegated specifically to the board of trustees, the AAUP *Statement on Government of Colleges and Universities* is widely considered the industry standard. In this erudite document, the organization states, "It should be noted that only the board speaks legally for the whole institution, although it may delegate responsibility to an agent. . . . The governing board of an institution of higher education operates in the United States, with few exceptions, as the final institutional authority. . . . The governing board has a special obligation to ensure that the history of the college or university shall serve as a prelude and inspiration to the future."[29]

Beyond these broad and generalized duties of governing boards, they are also responsible for selecting, evaluating, and firing of the president; fiduciary oversight; strategic planning, and personnel policies. Many of these responsibilities have operational delegation to the president.

The chief executive officer is charged with "the selection of academic deans and other chief academic officers . . . and determination of faculty status" in consultation with faculty governance.[30] On pages 3–4 of this same document, AAUP elaborates:

> The president shares responsibility for the definition and attainment of goals, for administrative action, and for operating the communications system. . . . The president represents the institution to its many publics. The president's leadership role is supported by delegated authority from the board and faculty. . . . As the chief planning officer of an institution, the president has a special obligation to innovate and initiate. . . . It is the duty of the president to see to it that the standards and procedures in operational use within the college or university conforms to the policy established by the governing board and to the standards of sound academic practice. *It is also incumbent on the president to ensure that faculty views, including dissenting views, are presented to the board. . . . Similarly, the faculty should be informed of the views of the board and the administration. . . .* [emphasis added]. The president is largely responsible for the maintenance of existing institutional resources and the creation of new resources.

In turn, presidents delegate operational responsibilities over to numerous professional leaders. Julie Carpenter-Hubin and Lydia Snover provide detailed descriptions of these officers and their corresponding responsibilities.[31] This list includes vice presidents and various directors and coordinators.

The third pillar, that is, the faculty, also have specified roles and responsibilities. Returning to the AAUP *Statement on Government* document referenced earlier, we find, "The faculty has primary responsibility for such fundamental areas as curriculum, subject matter and methods of instruction, research, faculty status, and those aspects of student life which related to educational process."[32] Other primary responsibilities include student admissions standards and whether graduation requirements have been met. As a matter of fact, most faculty senates have established a student admissions standing committee.

JOINT EFFORT

While each pillar has distinctive roles and responsibilities, the concept of shared governance works best when true sharing or collaboration occurs. This joint effort is described in great detail in numerous documents by the AAUP, the AGB, and the ACE.

Describing the thoughts of AAUP, Larry Gerber explained: "[I]n many areas of institutional decision making, such as long-range planning, budgeting, the setting of general education policy, and the selection of a president, the statement emphasizes the need for 'joint effort' and 'joint action' and the 'inescapable interdependence among governing board, administration, faculty, students, and others.'"[33]

Again, the AAUP gives us guidance on areas for joint effort. Faculty should have voice when it comes to the selection of the college president, in terms of short- and long-term planning, in terms of budgeting for curricular areas, and in terms of policies/procedures for salary increases.[34] AGB added, "Strategic issue-focused collaboration can take a variety of forms, such as task forces, advisory panels, working groups, and special committees. Such collaboration can provide an appealing avenue for meaningful interaction between board members and faculty."[35]

STAFF AND STUDENTS

For certain, the boards of trustees, college presidents, and the faculty are the three primary pillars of shared governance in higher education. Two other constituent groups surely have voices and roles in governance matters as well. These two groups include professional/support staff and the students themselves.

AAUP noted, "Ways should be found to permit significant student participation within the limits of attainable effectiveness. . . . Students expect, and have a right to expect, that the educational process will be structured. . . . If institutional support is to have its fullest possible meaning, it should incorporate the strength, freshness of view, and idealism of the student body."[36]

Two essays are included in this book, one each from both of these constituencies, expressing their involvement in shared governance in one private college. Descriptions of the roles of these distinct groups and their involvement in shared governance will be discussed later in this chapter and chapter 5.

One of the worst things that sink faculty and staff morale the most is serving on a committee that ultimately finds all of their hard work being ignored, or at least leaves that impression. It is imperative that different groups understand from the beginning their role in the decision-making process.

For example, do they make recommendations, do they advise, do they make final decisions, or are they involved purely for informational purposes only? Faculty and staff have far less issues with their work being decided against as long as they understand from the committee's inception that they are working in their present capacity to make recommendations only, than if they believed they were empowered with ultimate decision-making authority only to be overturned later.

The Pillar Responsibility Matrix (see Table 4.5) can serve as a broad parameter for each of the pillars. Each institution will, of course, need to adopt its own matrix, but this is a good framework from which to start. The Washington & Jefferson College Decision Matrix linked in the bibliography is an excellent example of one institution's attempt to do just that.[37]

In putting together the Responsibility Matrix, the members associated with each pillar need to keep in mind the principle of checks and balances and emphasize the focus on shared or joint decision-making when at all possible. The reader will note that the sample matrix shows very little unilateral decision-making and an emphasis on shared or joint decision-making.

For every topic, each of these constituent groups has a notation whether the individual or group has: unilateral decision-making authority, primary decision-making authority with input from other groups, consultation rights, or simply is informed. In some instances, the individual or group has no role.

The Washington & Jefferson College matrix indicates a place for "Approval." There will be times, for example, where the president may make a decision and the board of trustees must approve the decision. Likewise, there may be times when senior staff make a decision that needs presidential approval. When creating their own matrix, each college will need to determine how this issue is notated.

Should a college president think it would be wise to move academic programs, for example, to either an online or a hybrid delivery format, what should be the process for making the decision? The first question should be: Who has interest in the decision, and who has the competence do discuss it?

Table 4.5 Pillar Responsibility Matrix

	Responsibility Matrix			
Decisions	Site Council/Faculty Senate	Principal	District Council	Central Office/Board of Education
Planning				
Mission/Vision	SC4/FS4	P4		CO4/BE4
School Goals	SC4/FS4	P4		CO3/BE3
Strategic Planning	SC4/FS4	P4		CO3/BE3
Instruction				
Curriculum	FS4	P4		CO4/BE3
Assessment	FS4	P4		CO4/BE3
State/Fed. Regulations				CO1
Budget				
Operational	SC3/FS3	P2		CO3
Salaries				CO1
Merit Pay		P1		
Purchasing	SC3/FS3	P2		CO3
Personnel				
Hiring	SC3/FS4	P2		CO2
Staffing	SC3/FS3	P2		
Supervision	FS4	P4		
Evaluation		P1		
Staff Development	FS2	P3		
School Committees/ Operations				
Facility Use	SC3	P2		
Scheduling	FS3	P2		
Safety Guidelines	SC3	P2		
Discipline		P1		
Policies	SC4/FS4	P4		

(Continued)

Table 4.5 Pillar Responsibility Matrix (*Continued*)

	Responsibility Matrix			
Decisions	*Site Council/Faculty Senate*	*Principal*	*District Council*	*Central Office/Board of Education*
Democratic Integrity				
Annual Review of Governance Processes			DC	
Resolve Disputes			DC	

*A simple X could be placed along the row of each item listed in the matrix under the appropriate group. In most cases, decisions/items would need varying levels of cooperation from different groups, so a more nuanced system as shown in an abbreviated form below could be developed.

P1—Principal has unilateral decision-making authority. P2—Principal has decision-making authority with input from other groups. P3—Principal has input. P4—Principal shares responsibility with other group(s). SC1—Site council has unilateral decision-making authority. SC2—Site council has decision-making authority with input from principal or other groups. SC3—Site council has input. SC4—Site council shares responsibility with other group(s). FS1—Faculty senate has unilateral decision-making authority. FS2—Faculty senate has decision-making authority with input from other groups. FS3—Faculty senate has input. FS4—Faculty senate shares responsibility with other group(s). CO1—Central office has unilateral decision-making authority. CO2—Central office has decision-making authority with input from other groups. CO3—Central office has input. CO4—Central office shares responsibility with other group(s). BE1—Board of Education has sole decision-making authority. BE2—Board of Education has sole decision-making authority with consultation from groups. BE3—Board of Education has input. BE4—Board of Education shares responsibility with other group(s). DC—District council responsibility.

Clearly, the delivery format of curriculum falls under the purview of faculty. Further, the president is the leader of the academic institution. So, it would seem to be apparent that both should be involved in the decision, not only the discussion.

The board of trustees typically would not find curricular decisions in their area of responsibility. In this case, they should, however, definitely be made aware of such a decision if not involved in some form of discussions. On the other hand, if a significant portion of the academic program were to move away from traditional face-to-face delivery and go totally online, they would definitely need to be a part of the decision-making process.

Do staff council members have direct interest in the decision? As a council, probably not. On the other hand, there certainly are professional staff members who have expertise in such decisions (e.g., institutional effectiveness officer, technology specialists, etc.,). Likewise, students' views should be considered. Focus groups, open forums, and certainly representation on ad hoc committees would be most appropriate. It is worth the reminder that at times staff or students may not play a formal role, but they can be involved individually through an ad hoc process or committee.

Finally, in a 2016 white paper, the Association of Governing Boards wrote:

AGB's National Commission on College and University Board Governance recommended boards take steps to intentionally reinvigorate faculty shared governance. "Every board must ask for a review of the institution's policies and practices of shared governance with faculty in order to ensure that such policies are appropriate to the realities of the current workforce, reinforce the delegated authority of faculty for academic policy, and ensure that processes for consultation are clear and are routinely followed by all responsible parties. Boards must ensure that their policies for shared governance include means of addressing topics, presidential, and board responsibility (such as program closures)."[38]

From earlier in this chapter, we learned that the president and the board of trustees share primary responsibility or oversight for mission, planning, and financial resources/budgeting. The president also has primary responsibility for selection of deans and other administrators and has consultative responsibility with faculty for faculty status. At the same time, the board of trustees has oversight responsibilities for the president and personnel policies, and they have general review for faculty appointment, curricular decisions, and other academic matters.

Faculty have primary responsibility for curriculum, research, academic standards, and student life. At the same time, faculty should have consultative rights in the areas where the president and board of trustees have primary authority, namely planning, mission, and budgeting. Staff and student rights are more ambiguous in the literature, but most important in some necessary operational work and vision for the institution. These matters will need to be addressed as pillars negotiate their respective roles.

In terms of how decisions are made, Terrence MacTaggart shared the work of Heifetz, Vroom, and Jago. MacTaggart wrote: "Collaboration in making changes ranges from suggesting a few ideas to collectively arriving at a course of action. These definitions borrow from the thinking of management and leadership experts Ronald A. Heifetz, Victor H. Vroom, and Arthur G. Jago.

(1) **Unilateral action** occurs when one party or individual makes the call with minimal input from others;

(2) **Consultative processes** unfold when one party provides information to the other but does not share in making the decision;

(3) **Participatory modes** of involving groups in change invite more dialogue, and the issues discussed are more wide-ranging than in the consultative model. To participate in change implies a more equal relationship among the parties than in either the unilateral environment or the consultative relationship. Still, one party is the decider, and the other is not; and

(4) **Consensual approaches** mean that both parties discuss all the options and come to a mutually satisfying decision. This mode includes the consultative and participatory types of communication, but it goes further to result in genuine joint decision-making."[39]

In a similar fashion, the AAUP identified five categories for faculty involvement in decision-making: determination, joint action (formal), consultation (informal), discussion, or none.[40]

In a 2016 white paper entitled, "Shared Governance: Is OK Good Enough?" the AGB cited the work of Augustana College President Steven Bahls. Here, AGB noted, "Steven C. Bahls offers four perspectives on shared governance. . . .

A. **Shared governance as equal rights.** Shared governance ensures that faculty, staff, and administration have equal say in all governance matters, including budgets, academic directions of the institution, and strategic planning. Decisions are not made until a consensus is achieved.

B. **Shared governance as consultation.** Shared governance requires that those parties responsible for making decisions consult with others and consider their positions.

C. **Shared governance as rules of engagement.** Shared governance is a set of rules about the various roles and authority of the board, faculty, and administration is such things as academic decisions, budget decisions, selection of the president, and other operational decisions. Shared governance also describes rules of engagement when faculty, board members, and administration disagree.

D. **Shared governance as a system of aligning priorities.** Shared governance is a system of open communication aimed at aligning priorities, creating a culture of shared responsibility for the welfare of the institution, and creating a system of checks and balances to ensure the institution stays mission-centered."[41]

The following year, the AGB wrote another white paper entitled, "AGB Board of Directors' Statement on Shared Governance" outlining "threshold conditions for high-functioning shared governance" with the following six points:

- A shared commitment on the part of faculty, administration, and board members to the principles of shared governance.
- A shared and clearly articulated commitment to *trust, collaboration, communication, transparency, inclusiveness, honesty,* and *integrity* [emphasis in original].
- An institutional culture of good will, good intentions, and commitment to common values that is reinforced through the practice of shared governance.
- A shared commitment among all parties to focus the practice of shared governance on the institution's strategic goals, aspirations, and challenges.
- Constitutional documents that clearly codify decision-making authority as well as a thorough, nuanced understanding on the part of board members, faculty, and presidents of their own respective roles in shared governance, as well as those of their colleagues.
- A shared appreciation by board members and faculty of the complexity of the president's role in facilitating a constructive relationship between the board and the faculty.[42]

In 2017, the American Association of University Professors wrote:

Joint effort in an academic institution will take a variety of forms appropriate to the kinds of situations encountered. In some instances, an initial exploration or recommendation will be made by the president with consideration by the faculty at a later stage; in other instances, a first and essentially definitive recommendation will be made by the faculty, subject to the endorse of the president and the governing board. In still others, a substantive contribution can be made when student leaders are responsibility involved in the process. Although the variety of such approaches may be wide, at least two general conclusions regarding joint effort seem clearly warranted: (1) important areas of action involve at one time or another the initiating capacity and decision-making participation of all the institutional components, and (2) differences in the weight of each voice, from one point to the next, should be determined by reference to the responsibility of each component for the particular matter at hand.[43]

Before we continue with Sam's journey, we will read the insights and experiences of an individual who played a central role in taking student governance to a higher level—moving in the direction espoused by the principles shared in this book. The essay is written by a former two-term student government president.

STUDENT GOVERNMENT—KANLER CUMBASS

When I decided to run for Student Government Association president, I had already a good understanding of democracy. As we all know, those who desire office must first be elected by their student body. This basic principle is similar to that of the democratic republic we have in the United States. Ultimately, those who hold office in student government associations are representatives, and they are therefore part of a representative democracy. Student leaders are elected to represent the voice of their constituents.

So, once again, when I embarked on this journey, I had a clear understanding of my role—to represent students. But how? Often times, students are reminded to not hold positions within student government if they are looking for a so-called resume-filler. Yet, I believe that both administrators and students are responsible in determining whether or not a student's journey on SGA is one of a conversant, progressive nature or not.

It is easy for the students who run for these positions to come with fresh ideas on how to better student life for their campus. However, the challenge comes when the student seeks a voice with administration. For a student to be placed in a position where they are not just "filling their resume."

I believe the student must be given opportunities to exercise their voice. In this case, the institution must value democracy or shared decision-making. I believe it is important to have students serve on administrative committees or engage in open dialogue with senior level administrators. In simpler terms, to allow for true democracy or shared governance, the student leader must have a seat at the table and the opportunity to represent all students.

During my time as SGA president, I was invited to serve on a few committees. From these opportunities, I saw variations of democratic decision-making. It is important to note that these committees taught me "the politics" of higher education, how to best advocate, and how to be the administrator I will one day strive to be.

Politics in Higher Education

As I began my position as SGA president, I was quite unaware of the behind-the-scenes politics of higher education. It immediately became apparent to me that many faculty and staff members were on committees to solely represent their own departments. I was there to represent the students. This is when I began to really understand my role.

My job was to be the student representative. This was not easy. I sat alongside committee members who were faculty, staff, and administrators from various departments. Each member was different in their approach to committee work and had differing opinions on subject matter depending on which department they were there to represent.

First, there were those who were strong student advocates. These types of committee members often used vocabulary that suggested their willingness to have students' best interest at the front of their agenda. From my perspective, this type of administrator was extremely thoughtful in their decisions to support or not to support requests placed to the various committees. Meaning, this type of member often made decisions and asked questions based on data, research, students' best interest, and how it would particularly affect their department and the students within.

The questions they raised always concerned students. They sought my perspective and made me feel as if I was a valuable member of the team. This type of member was respectful of others in the room. They valued each representative and the principle of transparency. Even during disagreements, their desire to aid students and their level of professionalism did not waiver.

Second, there were members who I felt only represented their department without being conscious as to how their decisions would affect others on campus. Meaning, this type of administrator would only support requests made to the committee that would benefit their particular department.

Often times, these members made me feel uncomfortable as a student. Their intense style of representation did not allow for ideas to flow easily, nor would they easily hear a differing viewpoint before forming their own opinion and coming to a conclusion. They were always right (in their minds), and you could not convince them otherwise.

I must note that I am a student and these members have experience and knowledge beyond my years, but I must revert back to the concept of democracy. If we all played an equal role on the committee, wouldn't these administrators seek common ground? Better yet, wouldn't they seek to find opportunities to work together for the benefit of students? These are the questions I asked myself. Perhaps we truly weren't equal members.

An Example in Reality

This is where I began to understand the politics of higher education. Once, I served on the Student Technology Fee Committee. This committee was charged with distributing funds to departments across the campus with technology needs. During one of the committee meetings I witnessed two members raise their voices to an elevated level when discussing funding and how it should be distributed. I was confused, embarrassed, felt out of place, and knew that neither one of the members was truly advocating for students.

The argument was not about how the request would benefit students, but rather why one department deserved or did not deserve the funds for new technology on campus. My questions were: "How many students are in need of this new technology? If approved, how could we market our freshly acquired technology to new and incoming students? If we were to decline the request, how would we best explain the decision to those students who would be negatively impacted?"

Nevertheless, this was not the discussion the committee had. Finally, to end the heated discussion, the request was tabled. In my mind, I was thinking we are here to benefit students. We are here to distribute a fee that students pay, but instead we have prolonged the decision because of an unfortunate lack of professionalism and understanding of how to make meaningful conversation, dialogue, or, perhaps, debate.

I understand disagreements are natural. We will not always agree on how to distribute funds or develop a plan, but we must be skilled in crafting our response. Whether approving or not, we must be able to prove that the committee members are being good stewards of the fee that our students pay. On our campus, students were consistent in wanting to see results from the fee they were paying. Crafting a well-written response would allow for students to trust administration, but it would also keep the students updated as to how the funds were being distributed.

When I left that meeting, I was more disappointed in myself than in the members who engaged by arguing. I kept asking myself: "Why did you not speak up? You are there to represent the students." I was disappointed because I witnessed students being placed on the back-burner and I did not serve as their advocate. I also left with the understanding that one or two people can dramatically impact the dynamic and effectiveness of a committee.

What was I afraid of? Could it have been because of the faculty that served on this committee? I questioned the thought of upsetting one of them. Could they retaliate against me outside of this meeting space if I voted against one of their requests or challenged their ideas? If I were to explain how their actions made me feel uncomfortable, would I be deemed inferior and not fit to serve on this committee?

This was one of my first formal interactions with administrators as the SGA president. From that point forward, I became determined. I knew that it was not my responsibility to sit and watch others but to actively engage in the conversation myself, respectfully and with the will to learn.

How to Advocate

Later that year, the situation would arise again where two administrators would be on polar ends of a decision as to whether or not to approve a funding request. One of these administrators was the same as in the previous situation. As the conversation shifted, I spoke up.

Before the opportunity came for intense discussion, I asked the question: "Can we all take the time to read the charge of this committee again?" The room fell silent as we read aloud the committee's charge. The charge stated that we were seeking to provide new technology where there was a distinct need on campus. In attempts to redirect the conversation, I interjected, "I believe we should focus on the need. How great is the need? How many students would this impact?"

The conversation was redirected and the focal point was now on the need for new technology and how to positively impact students by the distribution of funds. I was proud of myself and knew that I had advocated for students in a respectful way. Indirectly, I asked the question, "What are we here for?"

With this story, I must note that I understand the situation is sometimes more complex and not as easy to solve, but as the student representative and voting member on any committee, my job was to help fulfill the charge of the committee. In this case, I completed that task. I learned a lot that day. I, as a student, was a form of accountability.

I used this learning moment to guide how I would advocate for students for the rest of my two terms. My focus was to help fulfill the charge of the committee or any goal set by administration. I utilized my senate to determine student satisfaction on decisions made by administration. Senators helped initiate meaningful conversation based on requests they received by students. We voiced these concerns and ideas to administration.

The purpose of my job was not to represent myself, but the entire student population, regardless of my personal perspective. My job responsibility included recognizing the institution's values and working alongside administration to better the day-to-day lives of students.

I recognized the importance of representative democracy. Before this point, I sat on the committee as a student, but I did not feel truly valued. Before that moment, I felt as if my seat at the table was for administration to say, "We have a student on the committee." I forced myself to play an active role.

Moving forward, I sought engagement with faculty and staff who actively listened to students. I appreciated the times when administrators began to look to me to provide feedback on how to address concerns. I found this type of environment when I served on the Quality Enhancement Plan (QEP) Steering Committee.

Throughout my time on the QEP Steering Committee, I learned about what it meant to be a professional in higher education. I was able to witness the development and implementation of our QEP. This committee, from the very beginning, involved students in the decision-making process. Our QEP director worked to create special positions that allowed students to serve on the QEP Steering Committee. These positions were called "student fellows." This offered opportunities for students to have face-to-face interaction with our leading administrators.

During each meeting, there was an agenda item dedicated to students. We were allowed to express concern, share ideas, and announce the projects we were working on. During this time, the committee would provide support in a variety of ways. The committee might offer advice, financial support, or even join our efforts.

I grew comfortable with the administration serving on this committee. We were mutually supportive of one another. Our QEP strategically and purposefully involved students and valued transparency during the process. No ideas brought forth by students were too abstract. Since the implementation of our QEP, an increasing number of students have become actively engaged in leadership, study travel, and undergraduate research.

I believe that our impressive involvement rates come from the fact that students were able to effectively market leadership, travel, and research opportunities. The administrators serving on this committee equipped us with the resources to become better advocates.

I must mention that we collected data on how many students we were able to reach throughout the series of outreach events we held. We designed outreach events and programs in order to educate other students about our QEP and high impact practices. We utilized the collected data to prove to administration ways that these events were impacting students. Through our student social media app, we allowed students to rate each event and provide additional comments. Administrators were intrigues to learn that our rating was high and our comments were all positive. This form of checks and balances held us all accountable.

The student fellows and I grew in our understanding of shared governance by serving on this committee. Before my time on this committee was over, I had reinvented myself. I entered college with the idea that I would attend law school after my undergraduate studies, but this committee was a true experiential learning model for me. I learned to love the challenge of higher education, how to involve students, and how to create a positive campus culture.

I was able to witness effective leadership. I felt valued. The committee members showed their appreciation to one another. It became apparent that everyone sitting in these meetings had one goal—to value the institution and all of its stakeholders.

From this experience, I started seeking ways to value democracy with my peers. The SGA began to have open-forum meetings about issues on campus. I wanted to allow students the opportunity to directly voice their concerns to the SGA and to the administration. I worked with my senators to change SGA policies. Now, our SGA allows for nonelected members to serve on any standing committee. These students do not have voting rights but are allowed to work with the committee chairs on special projects. This means any student who wants to be involved can be involved.

The SGA's goal was to provide students an opportunity to directly interact and work with their representatives. It was important for us to value transparency. Transparency, as I had witnessed, allowed for trust and meaningful relationships.

Final Thoughts

It is important to note that I have learned a great deal from each experience. I have grown tremendously from my position as student government president. For example, I understand that I want to pursue a career in Higher Education Administration. I also recognize who I will strive to be like, one day. Particular faculty, staff, and administrators have given me inspiration.

To students serving in a similar role as myself, I encourage you to seek opportunities to build connections. Collaborating with administration on projects can be intimidating, but you will be able to easily seek out those who are there to uplift and support you. I would encourage any student to embrace new challenges and to be bold in their leadership.

As mentioned before, I believe students' success in SGA is determined by both administration and the students, but the students must utilize each opportunity that they are given. Students should not slack in their efforts to better campus life. When provided a voice, use it. It is your job to be an advocate. If you are provided a seat at the table, it is because someone wants to hear you. Cherish collective decision-making.

Finally, I want to note that democracy is inclusive. Democracy allows for us to make decisions together. It allows for multiple parties to share their ideas and beliefs. Democracy is a beautiful concept, but only when used correctly and without manipulation from others for personal or political gain.

We should be thoughtful in how we include others in the decision-making process and recognize those who may be underrepresented. I have learned to uplift the values of democracy as I grow into a professional in the field of higher education.

SAM—JUST ANOTHER MANIC MONDAY

It was another Monday morning, and there were a number of things on Sam's agenda. There was to be a cabinet debrief about the HEMetrics forums, assorted appointments with an academic dean, two students, the Gen Ed Committee, and the follow-up chat with Beatriz and Camille. But, before all that Sam and the other vice presidents needed to attend a meeting with Henry Hutchins to discuss the budget. Sam had decided last week to send a quick email to her direct reports asking them to be careful on their expenditures in the near-term and to think of areas they could cut—just in case. She now left her office for the meeting with Henry and her colleagues.

Henry started by announcing, "I have some good news and some bad news. Which do you want to hear first?"

Sam looked around the room at the other faces. No one was smiling. Her colleagues all looked haggard. She then looked beyond the conference room table at Henry's shelves and walls. He had very few books to speak of, but he had plenty of reports, binders, and technical kinds of books. She noticed Sun Tzu's *The Art of War*.[44] It's a book she had never read before, but she had seen it on the shelves of other administrators before.

She saw a framed quote, in fact, on the wall behind Henry's desk. It read, "Let your plans be dark and impenetrable as night, and when you move, fall like a thunderbolt"—Sun Tzu. She also saw a framed C.P.A. diploma. But, she didn't see a college diploma, although Sam knew Henry had both a bachelor's and master's degree. She also noted that he had a Founder's football helmet on top of a filing cabinet. It looked like it was old-school—the kind with only one bar for a face mask.

Henry continued. "Alright. I'm afraid that word of our budget concerns has leaked out. Someone has told folks that we're in a budget crisis, that people were going to be laid off, and that significant cuts were going to be made." Sam wasn't certain, but it seemed like Henry looked at her the longest as he glanced around the table.

He added, "In fact, the good news is that there is no budget crisis. There need to be no layoffs or draconian cuts. Our negotiations with the health insurance company worked in our favor."

Sam felt a collective sigh of relief from her compatriots. She then blurted out, "I don't know if you were referring to me, Henry, but I did tell my people to simply be careful for now on their budgets. I thought it was the prudent thing to do. Folks continue to purchase things, and I just want to be careful. Each day will get more difficult to make cuts, if necessary."

"I understand, Sam," came Henry's reply. "But, my experience is that rumors spread quickly and get out of control just as quickly."

Peter jumped in, "On the other hand, my experience is that nature abhors a vacuum. Organizations abhor lack of communication. Where information is lacking, people fill in the blanks with their own information."

Henry concluded, "I guess it's a two-sided coin. Let's just make sure we're all working together as a team on this. The message to your reports should now be—our budget is on solid ground, and no layoffs or cuts. But, continue to be fiscally responsible, keep roughly 5% of your original budget in reserve, and there is a temporary hiring freeze until we see our spring enrollments."

To Sam this didn't really seem like good news. The vice presidents spent the next forty-five minutes clarifying Henry's points and discussing messaging parameters. It was then time to head to Lloyd's office to meet with Meng Xiong for the strategic planning debrief.

As they entered Lloyd's office, Meng was already there with a power point ready to share. Lloyd was out of the office today. He was often gone on Mondays visiting with a variety of donors, trustees, local business leaders, and even legislators.

Immediately, Sam identified the power point as a template prepared by the consultants with pertinent information about Founders University strategically placed throughout. It certainly made Sam think it was less than authentic, and she wondered how much would look the same for other colleges and universities. She dared not raise these thoughts aloud; Meng was serious in his presentation.

Meng noted that the plan neatly fell into three primary categories: students—support and enrollment growth; academics—contemporize existing majors and find new niche programs; and, revenue diversification and marketing/communication updating. Each vice president would serve as a cabinet lead and be responsible to put together university-wide and representative teams. A planning template included: goals, initiative objectives, individuals responsible, outcome and data metrics, budget and staffing, and timeline.

The model looked familiar; each planning firm really had their own spin on the same general approach. It reminded Sam of her college days sitting in Dr. Barnes' lectures on organizational management where he spoke of tightly coupled systems. Unfortunately, Sam knew such models worked best on paper and not in the real work world of loosely coupled systems described by Karl Weick. In any case, the chart gave clear focus and direction. Lloyd had set aside every other cabinet meeting with the sole focus of the strategic plan. People would be held accountable, that was to be sure.

In the afternoon, after a series of appointments, Sam was more than happy to leave her office and head to Camille's office. This meeting was actually called by Camille and Beatriz as a follow-up to their earlier conversation with Sam about creating a staff council. Sam brought in a cold cup of coffee; it was her thermos of morning coffee that she was never able to finish. She didn't mind, but this was happening more and more as the year wore on.

Camille started, "Sam, thanks for joining Beatriz and me. You really got us going. I have to admit, I was a skeptic at first but after talking to more people on campus I have found a lot of excitement. I really think we can do this."

Beatriz continued, "So, we have a cadre of about six of us who have been investigating what other universities do for staff councils. We've spent time visiting other institution's websites, we've called our counterparts at other schools, and Debbie Montgomery was actually a site council member at her previous college. She has been very helpful to us."

Sam was taken aback. These staff members, colleagues, had been doing all this investigating on their own—without her! As she was listening to their enthusiasm her emotions moved from "how dare they do this without me," to "this is precisely what should happen—they have taken ownership for their own governance." These feelings bounced back and forth over the next several minutes.

"We've started an ad hoc planning committee," Camille went on, "with each of us focusing on different areas. For example, we're looking at bylaws development, council structure, committee membership, recognition and communication, and responsibilities."

Beatriz interjected, "And, Sam, this is where we need you. There are three areas where we need you. We're likely going to need a modest budget, and we're also going to need some collective rights as a council—things that we'll be responsible for. This brings us to our third request of you. We'd like for you to serve as our administrative liaison to the President's Cabinet."

Sam's head was spinning. Was she losing control? Was this something she should be responsible to control? Well, yes, it was her idea and she told Lloyd about it. Lloyd told her to explore the idea and then present it to him. Camille and Beatriz had ideas, but what were they missing? And, she had no special funds budgeted for a new project, especially when a budget freeze was just shared.

Finally, "Yes. Yes, I can serve as your Cabinet liaison," Sam stammered. And, then she reminded herself of her fairly significant professional development budget. She knew there were funds that weren't spent last year, and she had very few fund requests to this point in the year. "Yes, I can set aside some monies for you, too."

With that said, they spent the next half hour jotting down structures, bylaws, and other ideas. Sam was going to use their hard work to help her prepare for her upcoming meeting with the president and his cabinet. But, in the back of her mind she had a nagging thought, "I have to keep on top of this and not let it get out of control."

It was 4:00 p.m. on a Tuesday afternoon. Sam found herself sitting in the large conference room of the faculty senate. As administrative liaison to the senate, Sam was a regular attendee. She sat at the table and had her own name plate in front of her. Her item was near the end of the agenda under New Business. This was going to be a long meeting waiting in anticipation of the discussion ahead.

It turned out that Sam really didn't have too much to worry about in terms of a long wait. There really wasn't much to discuss on the front end of the agenda; it was mostly just pro forma. Patrick McQuinlan introduced their joint topic.

Patrick began, "Vice President Sabbon and the Senate Executive Committee have discussed re-initiating our formal committee structures as established in our bylaws. In addition, the university is beginning a strategic planning process, and we need a seat at the table to play an active role as the institution moves forward."

Sam was pleased by the tone and assertiveness of Patrick. By the following discussion she could tell side conversations had already occurred and most senators were ready to join in. While Norman may have been reluctant to get involved in all this work, he did not attempt to dissuade the discussion. Rather, he encouraged all members to join the conversation and to share their thoughts. He didn't share his thoughts, but he let the process play out.

Before they ended the discussion, committee chairs were volunteered and elected. Each chair was to identify committee members, review their charges as established in the bylaws, and be ready to report at the next senate meeting. Sam was pleased and nodded quietly in affirmation.

The next morning had finally arrived. Sam was about to go to Dr. Sinclair's U.S. history class to open a dialogue about shared governance in higher education. As she was running her plan through her head, her phone rang. It was Vice President Hutchins.

Sam knew it was Henry as her phone screen showed the name of the caller. "Good morning, Henry. What's up?"

"Hello, Samantha. What's up with the Faculty Senate? Bernie Capell just called me and wants to schedule a meeting with me and his Senate Budget and Finance Committee. I didn't know we even had one. What do they want? What are they trying to do?"

Sam was not prepared for this series of questions. They almost felt like accusations. "Henry, the Senate is simply reconstituting their standing committees, committees that all colleges and universities have."

"Why didn't you give me a heads-up? Are they upset because of the budget announcements? What did you tell them?"

"No, no, no, Henry. Everything is fine. They just want to become involved in the strategic planning process, and it makes sense they would reconstitute their standing committees.

"Nothing is innocent," Henry mumbled. "We need to keep on top of this. I'm going to contact Lloyd and put this on the next agenda of the Cabinet."

"That's fine, Henry," Sam responded. "I was actually going to ask to put this on the Cabinet agenda, as well," replied Sam with a little white lie. "In any case, I have to run. I'm giving a guest lecture in Dr. Sinclair's class in two minutes."

"Better you than me," muttered Henry.

Sam walked into Dr. Sinclair's class. Every seat was occupied as he was a very popular instructor, and this was a Gen Ed class. Dr. Sinclair introduced Sam to his old college friend and software business CEO, Karl. Sam forgot about that. This amped up her adrenaline even more.

Dr. Sinclair actually took attendance. Every student was there. He then introduced Sam, turned the lectern over to her, and sat in a chair at the side of the room. She began by introducing herself and gave a little background describing just precisely what a vice president for academic affairs did. The students seemed rather nonplussed. She could tell she needed to dive into the topic quickly.

She looked out the windows at the back of the third floor classroom overlooking the academic quad. She saw the ivy-covered library looking stately as a single student walked in. She glanced up to the sky above the library where she saw a jet flying over leaving its exhaust contrail. "Man, I wish I were on that jet right now," she thought to herself. Then, she thought, "Focus, Sam! Focus!"

She began by asking the students to discuss democratic principles as laid out in the Constitution and the Bill of Rights. The students were better prepared than she anticipated. Of course, she thought to herself, this was Sinclair's class on U.S. history. She then pivoted to describing the corporate governance model. She gave a sideways glance toward Karl and treaded lightly as she was a bit uncertain on this topic.

Before talking of the three pillars and principles of shared governance in higher education, Sam asked the class who they thought would not like the ideas of shared governance in an organization. Several hands went up, but Sam called on a middle-aged, nontraditional male student sitting in the second row.

"From my experience, the people who argue against democratic decision making at work are those people who are in positions of power and authority. They feel they have the most to lose. They feel like they played by all the rules to get to the top, and now someone comes in and changes all the rules."

Wow, this guy was insightful. Sam used the moment. "Perfect. Let me expand on your thoughts. People in our organizations often say that they have no power. But, that's not true. They may not have formal authority, like the bosses, but they certainly have power. They have the power of their values, their beliefs, and their convictions. Even more, they have the power of those around them—their colleagues and friends and family. That is where our power comes from!" Sam often used this example in speeches, and she was quite pleased with her extemporaneous response.

The discussion continued for the next twenty-five minutes. Time was up before she knew it. The students actually gave Sam a short applause. Karl came up to her and said, "You really have given me something to think about. Maybe the business world could learn something from this discussion. I don't know. Maybe we are too dissimilar. Well, maybe we can talk some other time. Thank you, Dr. Sabbon."

After lunch, Sam only had one formal appointment on her calendar. This was a rarity. She was beginning to think she could catch up on the mounds of reading and report-writing awaiting her attention. Then came the knock at the door. It was her 1:30 p.m. appointment with Sammy McBride—a writer for the student newspaper.

Felicia Rhodes introduced herself enthusiastically, and immediately Sam felt at ease and she didn't feel Felicia would try any "gotcha" questions. They started with the obligatory questions and answers regarding background and goals for the year.

Felicia then made a comment that caught Sam's attention. "Dr. Sabbon, I also am a junior class representative on the Student Government Association. I heard you were thinking about making changes to student government."

Sam did not know how to respond. After a lengthy pause she said, "Well, I don't know about that. I have no plans. But, why do you ask? Are you asking as the reporter or as the S.G.A. representative?"

"Well, I guess both," came Felicia's reply. Then, she waited patiently for Sam to continue.

Sam didn't ask for this, but she didn't want to throw her colleague, Dirk, under the bus. Thoughts of recent conversations with her faculty and staff colleagues ran through her mind. She thought of her earlier dialogue with Dr.

Sinclair's class. "Really, Felicia, I'm not trying to make any changes; I don't have any plans. I know I would like to see the students more engaged in their university. Let me ask you, Felicia, are you happy with what the S.G.A.? Would you like to see changes?"

"To be honest, it feels more like our high school student council. We do some neat activities on campus, but really I don't think we do anything important. Our administration liaison, Mr. Zentkowski, kind of runs our student government."

Sam then asked Felicia another question, "What would you want to do differently, to see change?"

"Well, I'd like us to take more responsibility for our own agendas. I'd like to get students on university-wide committees," replied Felicia.

"What kinds of committees?," asked Sam.

"I don't even know what committees exist, Dr. Sabbon. But, I guess committees like the budget committee, the student fees committee, and maybe the admissions committee. I also heard that Founders is creating a strategic planning committee. That would be a perfect way for us to get involved, to get engaged."

Sam thought for a moment. "Felicia, I'm not your advisor, but I will be very happy to speak with him, as I believe this kind of work should come from him, not from me. How does that sound?"

Felicia nodded in agreement. "You know, Dr. Sabbon, my mother said I would like you."

"Oh, who is your mother, Felicia?"

Felicia replied, "Darlene Rhodes. She's a member of our Founders Board of Trustees. She was part of the committee that interviewed you."

"Oh, what a small world," uttered Sam quickly. She thought to herself, "What have I gotten myself into?" With that, Felicia and Sam spent another fifteen minutes finishing the actual interview for the student newspaper.

NOTES

1. Reinhold Niebuhr, *Reinhold Niebuhr: Major Works on Religion and Politics*, ed. Elisabeth Sifton (New York: Library of America, 1944, 354.

2. Patrick Dolan, *Restructuring our Schools: A Primer on Systemic Change* (Kansas City, MO: Systems and Organizations, 1994), 17.

3. "Constitutional Topic: Checks and Balances," (2005), 1–2, http://usconstitutio n.net/consttop_cnb.html.

4. Larry Gerber, *The Rise and Decline of Faculty Governance: Professionalization and the Modern American University* (Baltimore, MD: Johns Hopkins University Press, 2014), 9. The AGB "Statement on Board Responsibility for

Institutional Governance" went further: "Colleges and universities have a tradition of both academic freedom and constituent participation—commonly called 'shared governance'—that is strikingly different from business and more akin to that of other peer-review professions, such as law and medicine" as cited in Terrence MacTaggart, *Leading Change: How Boards and Presidents Build Exceptional Academic Institutions* (Washington, DC: AGB Press, 2011), 46.

5. Robert Birnbaum and Peter Eckel, "The Dilemma of Presidential Leadership," In *American Higher Education in the Twenty-First Century: Social, Political, and Economic Challenges* (Baltimore, MD: Johns Hopkins University Press 2005), 344. Two other authors, Schmidtlein and Berdahl, have extended these concerns:

> The characteristics of colleges and universities have led Etzioni to make a distinction between "administrative" and "professional" authority. This distinction has important implications for the tensions between the concepts of autonomy and accountability in higher education. Unfortunately, this distinction commonly is not understood nor, perhaps, appreciated by public officials who are more familiar with the "administrative" concept of organizational coordination and control and who believe that direct bureaucratic intervention can or should be able to, effectively alter academic practices in institutions.
>
> Schmidtlein, Frank, and Robert Berdahl, "Autonomy and Accountability: Who Controls Academe?" In Philip Altbach and Patricia Gumport, eds, *American Higher Education in the Twenty-First Century: Social, Political, and Economic Challenges* (Baltimore, MD: Johns Hopkins University Press, 2005), 71–72.

6. Robert Scott, *How University Boards Work: A Guide for Trustees, Officers, and Leaders in Higher Education* (Baltimore, MD: Johns Hopkins University Press, 2018), 6. Scott went further to quote Peter Drucker,

> Both the businessman and the civil servant tend to underrate the difficulty of managing service institutions. The businessman thinks it is all a matter of being efficient; the civil servant thinks it is all a matter of having the right procedures and control. Both are wrong—service institutions [such as universities] are more complex than either businesses or government agencies—as we are painfully finding out in our attempts to make the hospital [or university] a little more manageable. (Drucker in Scott 13)

7. Peter Block, *Stewardship: Choosing Service over Self-Interest* (San Francisco: Berrett-Koehler, 1996), 238.

8. Robert O'Neil, "Academic Freedom: Past, Present, and Future beyond September 11," In Philip Altbach and Patricia Gumport, eds, *American Higher Education in the Twenty-First Century: Social, Political, and Economic Challenges* (Baltimore, MD: Johns Hopkins University Press, 2005), 94–95.

9. Gary Olson, "Exactly What is 'Shared Governance'?" *The Chronicle of Higher Education* (July 23, 2009), 2.

10. William Bowen and Eugene Tobin, *Locus of Authority: The Evolution of Faculty Roles in the Governance of Higher Education* (Princeton, NJ: Princeton University Press, 2015), 85–86.

11. Bowen and Tobin, *Locus of Authority*, 86.

12. Ibid., 93–94.

13. Clark Kerr, "Governance and Functions," *Daedalus* 99 (1) (Winter 1970), 108–121. www.jstor.org/stable/20023936. Specifically, Kerr wrote: "The first is the heavy reliance on a board of trustees, regents, or managers composed of people drawn primarily from outside academic life and from outside governmental authority. . . . The second special feature is the comparatively strong role of the president, who is appointed without a specific term of office as a full-time executive with a relatively large administrative staff. . . . A third characteristic is the monolithic nature of the campus. . . . The fourth identifying trait is the importance of external, but nongovernmental forces in the conduct of the affairs of the campus," 108–109.

14. AGB, "AGB Board of Directors' Statement on Shared Governance" (Washington, DC: AGB, 2017), 11.

15. AGB, "Effective Governing Boards" (Washington, DC: AGB, 2014), vii. This same document went on: "The board works best when its members are confident that (1) the president displays true leadership; (2) the board remains focused on the institution's strategic priorities; (3) the board chair and the president have a good working relationship; (4) the president's cabinet is regularly welcomed into board conversations; (5) the faculty are meaningfully engaged in institutional governance; and (6) the board operates in a culture of cohesiveness, candor, transparency, and high ethical standards" (viii).

16. Kerr, "Governance and Functions," 108.

17. Olson, "Exactly What Is 'Shared Governance'?" 2.

18. Ibid.

19. Clara Chan, "A Common Plea of Professors: Why Can't My Faculty Senate Pull More Weight?" *The Chronicle of Higher Education* (July 6, 2017), 3.

20. Scott, *How University Boards Work*, 27–28.

21. Olson, "Exactly What Is 'Shared Governance'?" 1.

22. Ibid.

23. Brian Mitchell and Joseph King, *How to Run a College: A Practical Guide for Trustees, Faculty, Administrators, and Policymakers* (Baltimore, MD: Johns Hopkins University Press, 2018), 12. The same authors elaborated: "It comes down to leadership, which starts with the board of trustees. At the best-governed institutions, the groups understand their roles, including fiduciary, management, and programming duties of each group. This mandates what is typically a healthy tension. While shared governance fails for many reasons, the most likely cause is one group's overstepping its boundary," 13.

24. Rick Seltzer, "New Books Examine College Governance and How it can Adapt to Changing Times," *Inside Higher Education* (March 1, 2018), 1.

25. Scott, *How University Boards Work*, 27.

26. Ibid., 33.

27. Ibid., 28.

28. Mitchell and King, *How to Run a College*, 13.

29. AAUP, "Statement on Government of Colleges and Universities" (Washington, DC: American Association of University Professors, 2017), 3. www.aaup.org/report/statement-government-colleges-and-universities.

30. AAUP, "Statement on Government of Colleges and Universities," 3–4.

31. Julie Carpenter-Hubin, and Lydia Snover, "Key Leadership Positions and Performance Expectations," In Kristina Powers and Patrick Schloss, eds, *Organization and Administration in Higher Education* (New York, NY: Routledge, 2017), 27–47.

32. AAUP, "Statement on Government of Colleges and Universities," 4.

33. Larry Gerber, "College and University Governance: How the AAUP Has Established Widely Accepted Norms Shared Governance," *American Association of University Professors* (Washington, DC: AAUP, January–February 2015), 2, www.aaup.org/article/college-and-university-governance.

34. AAUP, "Statement on Government of Colleges and Universities," 4.

35. AGB, "Shared Governance: Is OK Good Enough?" (Washington, DC: AGB, 2016), 13.

36. AAUP, "Statement on Government of Colleges and Universities," 4–5.

37. Washington & Jefferson College Decision Matrix, American Council on Education (2017), www.acenet.edu/news-room/Documents/Washington-and-Jefferson-College-Decision-Matrix.pdf.

38. AGB, "Shared Governance," 21.

39. MacTaggart, *Leading Change*, 44. Citing the work of Ron Heifetz, 1994. *Leadership Without Easy Answers* (Harvard University Press, 1994), 121.

40. Gerber, Gerber, "College and University Governance," 101.

41. AGB, "Shared Governance," 3 (Bahls cited in this white paper). In a personal discussion with Dr. Bahls in Washington, DC in November 2018 he told me: "The best grade you can ever hope for in Shared Governance is a B."

42. AGB, "AGB Board of Directors' Statement on Shared Governance," 12.

43. AAUP, "Statement on Government of Colleges and Universities," 2.

44. Sun Tzu, *The Art of War*. 5th Century B.C. Translated in English by Lionel Giles in 1910.

Chapter 5

Back to the Future

Progress in America does not usually begin at the top and among the few, but from the bottom and among the many.[1]

Jon Meacham

"The future of shared governance, and of American higher education more generally, will be determined in large part by the extent to which an unfettered corporate-based market model continues to predominate in Americans' thinking in about every aspect of society."[2] Adding to this current state of affairs, Steven Bahls wrote, "The commitment to shared governance is too often a mile wide and an inch deep. Board members, faculty leaders, and presidents extol the value of shared governance, but it frequently means something different to each of them."[3]

With that said, the next iteration of shared governance must be more complex, more comprehensive, more ecological, and more robust, all out of necessity. More people will need to be involved in significant ways, and with more empowerment comes more responsibility and accountability. Shared governance is truly a two-sided coin.

Nothing can be made more clear than the Association of Shared Governance's proclamation: "Shared governance is complex. It requires action from multiple people serving in a variety of roles; regular policy review, habitual reflection on policy implementation, and ongoing dialogue should be sought by all involved and ensured by the board. One's sense of authority in a matter should closely follow one's accountability for the outcome."[4]

Stensaker and Vabo visualized the more rigid view of contemporary corporate models with more forward-leaning and dynamic democratic models. "The four possible models (representative democracy, corporate enterprise, collegial, and entrepreneurial) in which shared governance should be understood as ideal-type alternatives."[5] They elaborated:

> In the representative democracy model, emphasis would most likely be put on the close relationship between students, administration and academic staff in developing the institutions and the importance of, and respect for, formal rules and regulations for how decision-making processes should be organized. . . . In the collegial model, one would expect more emphasis on perceiving culture, ownership and decisions based on consensus. . . . In the corporate enterprise model, one could point out that representation of external stakeholders and actors in decision-making bodies would be seen as a vital characteristic. . . . Finally, one would expect that an entrepreneurial model of shared governance in strategic development processes would put much weight on the need for leadership and the discretion of dynamic leaders to take initiative and form coalitions for change and the creation of networks.

In citing the work of the president of Macalester College, Bowen and Tobin wrote:

> President Rosenberg has concluded that we should "rely more heavily for important decisions on representative rather than direct democracy." Here is his argument: . . . Better outcomes are likely to come from elected faculty committees whose members have the time and willingness to study complex issues. . . . One point is very clear to us. In thinking about "representative governance" models, careful attention needs to be paid to how members of a faculty senate (or some such body) are chosen. Both nomination and voting processes need to be designed to ensure, as best one can, that able individuals are chosen from various parts of the body politic.[6]

For certain, there are some requisite conditions necessary to implement such shared or joint governance protocols. "A college can move forward only if those who run it are educated about the work they do, know their responsibilities, respect their role and those of those who also lead, and create measures by which to demonstrate their effectiveness."[7]

In a similar vein, the AGB stipulated, "Along with presidents, boards can collaborate with faculty more often on substantive matters. Presidents can promote strong shared governance by ensuring that boards and faculty understand the work of the other and its value to the institution."[8] In any case, eminent scholar of higher education, Clark Kerr, concluded: "Area by area, the central questions should be who has an interest in the problem and who has competence to deal with it."[9]

A new contemporary model of shared governance or joint effort requires a new way to understand organizational structures. Kezar and Holcombe call for a new understanding of "shared leadership," as well. "Shared leadership is more flexible in identifying expertise, noting that various individuals on campus might have expertise. . . . All perspectives are drawn in and decisions are not delegated purely to a single group; rather, collaboration across groups in decision making is emphasized. Shared leadership is also associated with adaptable and flexible decision structures, rather than the fixed structures common to shared governance such as faculty senates."[10]

The Association of Governing Boards echoed these findings, noting:

[B]oards and presidents are often finding that the formal committee structure of the board . . . is not well suited to addressing the major strategic challenges and opportunities facing them. . . . An increasingly common practice in addressing these major issues is the creation of task forces composed of those with the experience and expertise to best explore the issue and options, and make recommendations to the board and the administrative leadership. The task forces (or *ad hoc* committees) often include membership of other stakeholders in addition to board members—administrators and staff, faculty, and students, depending on the nature of the issue.[11]

Stensaker and Vabo remind us that this would necessitate a move from a more "pure corporatist business-like model . . . to more representative democracy models."[12] The understanding is that the context is different in a professional organization vis-à-vis a for-profit organization; hence, the need for a different governance structure. Further, our contemporary organizations need to be more nimble and responsive to needs. Each circumstance might require different leaders to emerge to meet these needs. Lipman-Blumen posited:

Unlike the rigid hierarchies of formal organizations, the informal system may be compose of many loosely structured webs, outside the change of reporting channels. More flexible than hierarchies, network segments can operate separately. They even break away temporarily for specific purposes and then regroup without damage—sometimes in new configurations.[13]

This note should not infer that the formal organizational shared governance structure must change, but this flexible approach may be a way for faculty, staff, students, and other constituents to have a voice and share their expertise. In other words, a fluid and adapting system needs to be allowed and encouraged within the formalized structure.

To put a finer point on describing the rational for this new model, noted natural scientist Fritjof Capra talks of a need for balance between bureaucratic and organic structures. He calls these "designed structures" and "emergent structures," respectively. These two types of structures are very different and every organization needs both kinds:

Designed structures provide the rules and routines that are necessary for the effective functioning of the organization. . . . Designed structures provide stability. Emergent structures, on the other hand, provide novelty, creativity, and flexibility. They are adaptive, capable of changing and evolving. In today's complex business environment, purely designed structures do not have the necessary responsiveness and learning capability. They may be capable of magnificent feats, but since they are not adaptive, they are deficient when it comes to learning and changing, and thus likely to be left behind.[14]

And, of course, with increased empowerment and involvement in shared or joint participation comes the associated shared and joint responsibility. With the understanding of joint or shared responsibility must be an inherent sense of commitment to one another, to the other constituents.

Bowen and Tobin stipulated, "[S]hared governance should be viewed, not so much in terms of 'who owns what,' but as embracing a commitment to a genuine sharing of perspectives. . . . accompanied by a recognition that nimble decision-making is required. Nimbleness implies a need for a well-understood locus of authority, with administrators expected to listen carefully to those with ideas and expertise to contribute."[15]

Recognizing the ever-present desire to quicken the pace for expedient decision-making, Baldwin suggests a number of formal and informal interactions among the shared governance groups to mitigate these concerns. "Ideally, thoughtful board-faculty dialogue can lead to more realistic policies and practices that do not ignore or overlook the complexities of difficult points of view that should be considered when a difficult problem such as tuition policy or student attrition is considered."[16]

Ultimately, such collaborative efforts will "make higher education more accountable to external stakeholders, as shared leadership enables institutions to create meaningful and lasting changes in organizations."[17] With all this said, historical, and even conventional, animosity toward one another makes initial steps into open dialogue difficult. Building trust will be key.

> [T]rust takes time to build, implying that "consultations" with academic staff has to be perceived as something more than just a symbolic process where it might be difficult to create a balance between speed and efficiency on the one side and trust and engagement on the other. . . . One option for solving this challenge is to clarify key principles, norms and values, *a priori* specific decisions that have to be taken, creating a kind of social contract between the academic staff and the leadership on how certain issues are to be tackled.[18]

These a priori norms should be built into the Pillar Responsibility Matrix described in chapter 4 and enumerated in table 4.5. Such contemporary models of joint decision-making and responsibility will require new understandings of leadership and appropriate training. Members of all groups need to better understand not only their own roles in decision-making but the roles of the other pillars, as well.[19]

In a survey of college presidents, "[O]nly about 30 percent . . . reported that the typical board member understands the work of the faculty well or very well, and only about 20 percent said that the typical faculty member understands the work of the board well or very well."[20]

Mitchell and King provide a particularly erudite description of expectations of each of the pillars, particularly of boards, board chairs, and presidents. These authors explain that transparency is a central feature to shared governance and that board members need to fully understand the differences between corporate governance and higher education governance and the work of the other pillars.[21]

With this said, roles of these pillars are becoming more complex. Boards need to move from corporate-style thinking to one of shared expertise. As Robert Scott stated, "Universities should be focused on transformations, in terms of knowledge, skills, abilities, and values, not on transactions."[22] They need to consider themselves partners and collaborators; they need to make certain the principles of shared governance are being followed.

On the flip side of this coin, many board members feel important decisions and discussions have already been made prior to board meetings. In other words, they feel they have not been consulted or listened to—their voices never heard.[23] This is where the president needs to step in and make certain the board is involved appropriately, not just as a rubber stamp.

Not only should the president, as a matter of routine, meet with individual trustees, the president should also meet regularly with individual faculty members and their representatives, with their staff and, of course, their senior administrators. Presidents should also meet with regularity student government representatives, members of the student newspaper, and others in order to keep them informed and to listen to their concerns.[24]

While the relationship between the board and the president is the foundation for successful change, it is essential to engage the faculty in serious dialogue when the change involves fundamental issues like mission, strategic direction, curriculum, programs, or various aspects of the teaching-learning model. When it comes to genuinely improving academic programs, making the student learning experience richer and more challenging, and redesigning the curriculum, there is simply no way to do it without the teaching faculty.[25]

It will be critical that the areas of faculty oversight are not lost in our rush for expediency in decision-making and to not delegate their authority to administration.[26] In extending this thought, Stephen F. Eisenman—former president of Northwestern University's faculty senate noted, "An active, engaged faculty senate is crucial for a university to be progressive and dynamic and innovative. You want a university where new ideas are generated from the ground up, not from the top down. . . . It certainly causes more controversy, and the arguments—disputes of all kinds—will be messy, but that messiness is where new ideas, innovation, and progress happens."[27]

The AGB states the faculty "[s]ervice on institution-wide committees may be the most promising area for substantial interaction."[28] One particular area of contemporary import for direct faculty engagement is the movement for online instruction. Bowen and Tobin state four areas for this professional involvement: decisions in platforms; the uses at "home" of the technology; the sharing of technology across institutions; and, curricular development involving the degree of blending approaches.[29]

On the other hand, Bowen and Tobin caution of faculty overreach. For example, faculty should not be involved at the decision-level for the closure of programs and corresponding resource allocation.[30] These same authors concluded:

> [t]hree things are clear to us: (1) Faculty cannot be given a veto over the introduction of new approaches to teaching content, and we do not think that, with proper incentives in place, many faculty would expect such veto power. . . . (2) Faculty expertise and faculty enthusiasm are indispensable to finding cost-effective ways of delivering excellent educational content. Absent significant faculty involvement in designing, customizing, and implementing new approaches, frustration and, yes, failure are inevitable. (3) College and university presidents must engage (or re-engage) in academic matters.[31]

Larry Gerber gives one final warning of the express need for active faculty involvement in any governance structure. "In the case of higher education, a professional professoriate acting through the mechanisms of shared governance is potentially the last-line defender against the triumph of a narrowly utilitarian definition of the purpose of higher education that views students as customers and sees job training as the sole function of colleges and universities."[32]

Today's professional staff members also must have a voice in emerging models of joint decision-making. Their trained expertise and experience are invaluable assets to the mission of the institution and must be relied upon for advice across the spectrum in final decision-making. The same can be said for alumni and various advisory groups. In his must-read book, *Restructuring Our Schools: A Primer on Systemic Change*, Patrick Dolan showed his vision for their involvement in current bureaucratic structures.[33] (See figure 5.1).

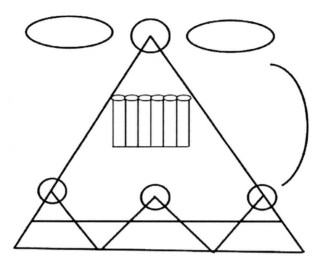

Figure 5.1 K–12 School System Governance Pyramid. *Source*: Patrick Dolan. 1994. *Restructuring Our Schools: A Primer on Systemic Change.* Kansas City: Systems & Organization. 65.

In Dolan's depiction of contemporary school systems, he shows a classical pyramid model. At the top is the superintendent—along the sweeping arc are the other two anchors: the board of education and the teachers union. Below the superintendent are various central office administrators and administrative units. Below those are the various schools—each with their own micropyramids with principals atop. Along the side of the pyramid is another sweeping arc indicating a place for outside constituent groups.

It is easy to see this same K–12 model depicting traditional higher educational governance structures with the president at the top of the pyramid and the board of trustees and faculty senate along the top arc. Administrative units fall immediately under the president, and under them the various schools or colleges as micro-pyramids. Students and staff constituents would belong on the outer arc.

Likewise, emerging models of joint leadership are engaging students to a much larger extent. Robert Scott has written to the need for the role of students in shared governance.

> While it may not be appropriate to include students as voting members on a board, including the president of the student government association and several representatives from the student body on the board's student life committee can be helpful. The board can also organize opportunities during lunch or dinner meetings to hear from students about special achievements and concerns.[34]

The voice and insights of students is crucial for decision-making in higher education. Again, Robert Scott elaborates:

> For boards and presidents, the most important priority should be student success. Therefore, the board should know the goals for student retention from year to year and to graduation. They should know the goals for licensure exam results . . . and financial aid policies. . . . Other questions relate to the adequacy of plans for controlling student indebtedness and federal financial aid default rates. How are admissions standards set in order to achieve both the goal for diversity in the student body and for graduation rates for those who are admitted?[35]

One final note on the leadership of boards of trustees, as they are the ultimate arbitrator of all consequential decisions made at a college. These people need to be selected with care and for certain characteristics. "Strong, effective, and moral leaders and trustees are needed to serve as a voice representing the enduring values of higher education."[36] In addition, board members are selected for their expertise and for their commitment to the values and vision of the institution, not as representative of particular constituencies.[37] In that spirit:

> Boards of independent colleges and universities should regularly review and renew their composition, with an eye to such factors as diversity by race, gender, geography, and occupation; financial expertise or literacy; experience within the community of higher education; independence; knowledge of or affinity with the institution; commitment to personal philanthropy and recruitment of other donors; and enthusiasm for trusteeship as a voluntary commitment.[38]

Finally, Mitchell and King describe the necessity of careful consideration of the leader of the board of trustees—the chair.

> In shared governance, the ringmaster is the chair of the Board of Trustees. When selecting a new board chair, the board should always seek experienced, competent leaders who are devoid of an agenda. Before they are selected, *board chairs should be as carefully vetted as a new president* [emphasis added], moving steadily through different board leadership positions as they progress toward the chairmanship. Furthermore, they should have a collegial and effective working professional relationship with the president and key faculty leadership.[39]

Citing the National Commission on College and University Board Governance, Robert Scott noted several characteristics of "consequential" boards. One of particular note follows: "They improve shared governance through attention to board-president relationships, re-invigoration of faculty shared governance, and leadership development for the board, the president, and faculty senate officers."[40]

In 2014, Steven Bahls wrote for AGB of five practices "when deliberately followed, create the alignment in which administrators, board members, and faculty members become integral leaders:

(1) Actively engage board members, administrators, and faculty leaders in a serious discussion of what shared governance is (and isn't).
(2) Periodically assess the state of shared governance and develop an action plan to improve it.
(3) Expressly support strong faculty governance of the academic program.
(4) Maintain a steadfast commitment to three-way transparency and frequent communication.
(5) Develop deliberate ways to increase social capital between board members of the faculty."[41]

This was followed in 2017 when the AGB identified four principles of shared governance:

- Boards should commit to ensuring a broad understanding of shared governance and the value it offers an institution or system;
- For shared governance to work, it must be based on a culture of meaningful engagement;
- Shared governance requires a consistent commitment by institutional and board leaders; and,
- Institutional policies that define shared governance should be reviewed periodically to ensure their currency and applicability.[42]

WHERE DO WE BEGIN?

Such a journey into a new model of shared governance will take both courage and forward thinking; it will take leadership. Those at the top of the current structure—the three pillars—will need to agree that such an endeavor is necessary, and they must become active participants—this means the chair of the board of trustees (or an executive designee), the president, and the faculty senate president (or designee). After common understanding begins to develop among these three pillar leaders, only then can leaders from the other constituents (e.g., staff and students) enter the dialogue as partners.

As this is not a corporate model, but rather one that is more akin to a democratic model, they will need to agree on core values for democratic decision-making. For example, we learned from the Declaration of Independence that all people are created equally and that the leaders receive their power and authority from their constituents. We also learned that five core democratic values include liberty, common good, justice, equality, and diversity.

Further, we are reminded of four constitutional principles as they relate to the workplace. These are rule of law, separation of powers, representative government, and checks and balances. In addition, we learned that the First Amendment in the Bill of Rights spoke to the necessity of freedom of speech and assembly. We need to keep this seminal ideals in mind as we frame our structures, roles, and processes.

After these core values and principles are agreed upon, the next step would focus on review of the three branches, or pillars, and the responsibilities of each. While these three pillars already exist, their functions and responsibilities need to be reviewed. Concurrently, a discussion would need to begin as to the responsibilities and roles of students and staff, most likely represented through the SGA and a staff council, respectively. The Pillar Responsibility Matrix would provide the necessary framework for these deliberations.

Preliminary discussions among each representative group would be the next appropriate step. Board members, senior cabinet members, faculty senate, SGA, and professional staff members would need to learn about this new endeavor, to ask questions, and to provide feedback. They need the time and space to have their own internal dialogue.

This would be an iterative process, but it would be important to not lose momentum by letting discussion get bogged down in minutia. No model will be perfect. As Winston Churchill famously stated, "Democracy is the worst form of government, except all others." This model must not be static; rather, it must be malleable—a living structure that can grow, change, and improve over time. Therefore, an annual review of policies and practices must occur in order to determine the extent to which the principles and values remain intact.

After these feedback sessions are agreed upon, policies and protocols will need to be codified and approved by the board of trustees. At the same time, the role of alumni and advisory groups will need to be considered. Patrick Dolan's depiction captured in figure 5.1 would be worth consideration.

In addition, at a minimum, on an annual basis the new system will need to be reviewed to make certain it is adhering to the democratic values and principles espoused at the outset. For example, is the Pillar Responsibility Matrix being followed (and, do adjustments need to be made), is transparency being followed, is open dialogue encouraged and not punished, do any of the pillars overstep their bounds, is there equity and diversity in representation, and so on. Table 5.1 Democratic Principles Matrix could serve as a framework for this investigation.

The journey of a thousand miles begins with a single step, as does creating a new culture. Let us begin by talking about talking. Democratic decision-making processes and dialogue are requisite central features to any institution

Table 5.1   Democratic Principles Matrix

Democratic Principles Matrix			
Principle	*Meets Expectations*	*Making Good Progress*	*Needs Improvement*
Checks/Balances			
Separation of Power			
Representation			
Communication			
Transparency			
*Comments:			

that chooses to provide the critical praxis and dialectic as defined by Paulo Freire.[43] People who enter this dialogue need to feel safe to share their questions and concerns without fear of retribution. This is most true for the faculty, staff, and students.

Critical dialogue is the vehicle for practitioners to become aware of their condition, their promise, and the path to get there.[44] "The issue raised for organizational communication scholars is how to design a structure that integrates wider participation and provides for the expertise required for effective decision making."[45] Viviane Robinson elucidated as to how this is to be accomplished:

> Participants in a problem-solving discourse must be committed to three discourse values. The first, that of respect, ensures . . . fair opportunity to speak, to challenge or continue any line of inquiry, to express one's feeling and to be in general unconstrained in one's with the other parties in the discourse. The second discourse value is that of commitment to valid information. It involves the commitment to the conduct of discourse in ways that increase the chances of detection of error in one's own and other's claims about the nature of the problem and how to solve it . . . they welcome rather than discourage different perspectives. . . . The third value, that of commitment to the promise and outcomes of dialogue . . . involves being motivated to expend the intellectual and emotional effort required until all parties to proclaim to each other and to third parties that they have a solution that is the best they can construct, given their mutually agreed constraints on the problem.[46]

Therefore, it will be critical for college leaders who espouse democratic values to create opportunities (both in terms of time and place) for faculty, staff, students, alumni, and other constituents to begin the dialogue about their values, participatory roles and commensurate responsibilities, and the way forward.

Such conversations will not be one-time in nature, but this will necessitate an iterative process and opportunities to bring diverse groups together to share in the dialogue. Indeed, running such interactions will demand different types of skills of our emerging democratic leaders.

These leaders will need to "give strong leadership. Not strong in the sense of authority, but in terms of strength of purpose, of holding to your democratic values even when things get difficult. Tenacity and humility in a leader call for greater strength of character than the exercise of power."[47]

Students' voices will need to be heard as they begin to take more ownership and responsibility for their own education. This does not mean the students vote on the curriculum, the content, or the pedagogy, but their voice needs to be heard. They need a seat at the table of their own education. There will be formal roles on standing committees and informal roles on ad hoc committees. Students should speak at student affairs committee meetings every time boards of trustees hold full board meetings.

Roles of the students will not be the only ones that need to be reexamined and changed. Clearly, the roles of the president and the board of trustees will necessarily see significant change. Present governance models have the executive deriving their power from their positional authority. A more democratic or joint model will shift the primary focus of power from one derived through formal position to more the individual's ability to relate, to empower the process and the constituent groups, and to persuade—to truly lead.

Board members will need to be trained as to their roles and responsibilities, as well as the culture of higher education. They will need to understand the significant differences between corporate boards and higher education boards. The most essential read is: "Effective Governing Boards: A *Guide for Members of Governing Boards of Independent Colleges and Universities.*"[48] This monograph can serve as a template for board training for those members who are committed to shared governance.

Trustees will need to be mindful of process, to make certain that democratic principles are being followed and that slippage back into the old order does not occur. In order to make sound decisions, these newly involved groups will need information—information that has traditionally only been under the purview of administration. They will also need to understand that with these new freedoms come new responsibilities in terms of time commitment, to the democratic values of shared decision-making and to the very processes of democratic decision-making.

It should be reiterated that democratic decision-making processes don't require people or groups to vote on everything. Quite often all that is truly necessary is the opportunity to share in dialogue, have information available, and to have decisions made in a transparent fashion.

If we keep some seminal values and principles in mind on this journey, we will be in good stead. These ideals are: authority and power comes from the governed; the values of liberty, common good, justice, equality, and diversity; and the collective understanding of the rule of law, separation of powers, representative governance, checks and balances, and freedom of speech and assembly.

One final thought is appropriate, here. All groups involved in a shift to more democratic or joint governance will need to be mindful about the process of change. Most notably, it will take time—time to develop and the precious time of participation—and patience. Such a human endeavor, a culture shift, will not go smoothly. Those who feel they will be losing power will fight to change the fiercest. Likewise, this endeavor must not be seen as a form of manipulation by those in authority—"the iron fist wrapped in a velvet glove."

Our final essay before we conclude with Sam's journey. This essay was written by an associate dean of student life. She was instrumental in training and leading students in taking student government to a meaningful level. The students found their voice, became campus leaders, and truly started to become an important asset to shared governance at their college.

STUDENT GOVERNMENT—KIM CRAWFORD, EDD

Developing students into compassionate leaders is part of my institution's liberal arts college mission. The institution attempts to prepare leaders who pursue innovation and ethics while also providing them opportunities to experience transformative and reciprocal learning. At its core, these values and goals provide much direction for the students as well as the faculty and staff that work here.

However, over the past few years, students have just begun to find their voice on campus. Before I took this position as an administrator in higher education, the students were not given the guidance, direction, or training to help instill basic democratic principles or given direction about the importance of advocacy.

In fact, students were struggling with being homesick, lonely, and lacked knowledge of self-advocacy and the concept of shared decision-making. They were focused on how they were feeling and not about how they could serve others or how they could impact their campus community by exercising their democratic voice.

Students on campus were learning in the classroom, but they did not exactly understand how to apply basic democratic principles or even exercise their student voice outside the classroom to address how administration was making decisions. In addition, administrators were making decisions for students, but not inviting them to participate in the decision-making process or providing any transparency for how decisions were being made, which left students in limbo.

As student affairs professionals focused on helping students develop themselves as leaders, it was time to revisit what the cocurricular programs included in order to ensure students were given the opportunity to feel empowered and that they too could have a voice.

This realization included providing students hands-on training and supervision of one of the main student organizations on campus, the SGA, as well as advocating for students to serve on committees at the institution.

The leadership workshops provided students the chance to participate in conversations about advocacy and what that looked like in regard to advocating for oneself as well as others. In these training sessions, students were challenged to think outside of their typical frames of reference. They were asked to consider what someone else's experiences were like and how to articulate their needs to others.

These conversations led to deep discussions about identity and ultimately led to much self-reflection, which allowed growth in the students' ability to find their voice. This along with educational workshops that explored personal strengths allowed students to reflect on themselves and provided opportunities for them to explore the qualities that make them unique.

In addition, accepting and understanding the different aspects that make up an individual's identity was a new process for them, but it gave them confidence to speak up. This began the groundwork for student leaders to be prepared to be part of the decision-making process. These trainings allowed students the opportunity to discover themselves as leaders and as democratic citizens that could directly impact their campus and global communities.

Allowing students to begin with internal reflection led to confidence in who they were as individuals and as leaders. This process led to self-realization that they were accepted by the institution and free to be who they were. This was the foundation to the confidence needed in order to empower and cultivate the student voice.

While this was taking place, administrators began to expand opportunities for students to serve on additional discussion panels, committees, safety groups, and other task forces on campus. This was the first time there was transparency provided in the decision-making process and showed the institution was beginning to value the student voice.

Once students were given a seat at the table, they began to feel empowered to speak up for what they believed was right or fair. At first, they sat back and listened to the discussion as well as the opinions of other administrators. Then, when they felt comfortable they began to speak to administrators about what they felt students wanted to see on campus.

As institution-wide decisions began to take shape, student affairs advocated for the need to allow students opportunities to have a voice at the decision-making table. The need to allow students to exercise their rights was evident.

It was important for students to feel as though they had shared governance in institution-wide decisions. Soon thereafter, they were given the opportunity to be part of the planning for our Quality Enhancement Plan (QEP) and the Technology Committee.

For the first time, the institution viewed students as stakeholders who should be part of decision-making processes where they were asked their opinion on certain decisions. While students had the opportunity to hear discussion before decisions were made, they quickly learned how difficult it was to please administrators, students, and other campus partners and stakeholders.

The SGA president served on the planning committee for the QEP, and students at the institution were given for the first time a seat at the table in order to advocate for the student voice on campus. They also helped create buy-in from students, which gave administrators confidence in their ability to lean into student support.

At the same time, a technology fee was implemented and a committee was formed in order to discuss how to properly spend those resources to provide top-of-the-line technology for students. Two students were given the opportunity to serve on that committee along with administrative representatives across disciplines and departments at the institution.

Allowing students the space and place, such as serving on committees, to have a voice and be part of the shared decision-making process provided them a firsthand look at how decisions were made. They were given the freedom to exercise their voice, which was beginning to be accepted by the campus community. This experience allowed for more balance of influence between students and administration.

Another space students were given to have a voice was our campus app. Within the app, there is a social area space, called the campus wall, where students can provide comments in a more social way. While this is monitored by administrators, students have the freedom and the space to voice concerns about things taking place on campus.

This place also provides an outlet for students to safely express how they feel about decisions or changes on campus in a way that introverts and extroverts can express themselves freely.

Their voice or vote was not always greeted with a welcoming environment, but that did not keep students from speaking up. This allowed administrators for that first time on campus to hear from students and not just to guess what they thought students wanted. It was the first time administrators stopped to formally ask their constituents how they felt about issues, which was powerful. It was a way for administrators to appear transparent in making decisions and gave students confidence in their ability to have a voice in decisions being made on campus.

Even though they did not always agree with decisions or support what administration was proposing, and did not even feel welcomed by all of those sitting at the table, the ability to be part of the conversation was all it took to create a spark in them to continue to feel empowered. They quickly learned how to articulate their ideas to administrators and learned how to work alongside them in order to build a professional working relationship with those that they needed to.

Culture Shift

Changing the culture to include students as part of the process was a new concept to bring forward. As a new professional at the institution, I myself struggled at times to have my voice heard. I had not been there long and felt like even asking questions to current administrators was sometimes viewed as taboo.

However, as an administrator at the institution working alongside students and upper-level administrators, I also worked hard, served on committees and advocated for students and their voice whenever I could. I took time to invest in the students on campus in order to earn their trust so I could ask them what we could do as an institution to improve and help them to feel a sense of belonging.

This philosophy of student development, coupled with hands-on and continuous leadership training and support, led to the main student liaison group on campus—the SGA—the ability to find their voice in shared governance. The level of care taken to work hard and to earn the trust of both administrators and the students was important for me since I felt that a foundation must be built in order to even try and create a platform for student democracy and advocacy.

Students embraced the challenge to speak up in a way that administration would listen. They worked hard to build rapport with area deans and vice presidents to earn their trust. Leaders worked to improve their leadership skills. They were willing to listen to understand and not just to respond or react in a way that would not give them a voice.

Student Rights

Students have the right to advocate for themselves and others, but often they must be given training and the space to do so. These spaces to have a voice could be in the form of surveys, town hall meetings, and serving on various committees on campus. They have to properly request the opportunity for consultation. In addition, they have a right to be aware of things and a right to have transparency from administration.

I think they also have the right to voice their concerns to the SGA who should be part of the decision-making processes especially when the decision directly impacts students. This could include things such as financial changes for textbooks, tuition, technology on campus, or new third spaces on campus.

Students also have the right to serve on as many committees possible in order to accurately and appropriately represent the student voice and the overall student body at higher education institutions. A student voice from student groups such as SGA should always be invited to send a representative.

Democratic principles cannot just be taught. Student voices must be viewed as valuable to the institution before decisions are made for them. Instead of assuming faculty and staff know what students want and need, they must actually take the time to ask students' opinions about certain topics that are being considered. This creates buy-in as well as true transparency.

Opportunities must be present that allows students to voice their opinion whether that be serving on a committee or by joining a student group on campus such as the SGA that is charged to help students navigate the proper channels and bring student concerns forward. These experiences also provide a living laboratory for students to experience democracy in action.

In addition, upper level administrators must respect and consider the important part students play in making decisions that impact the institution in order for a shared governance to truly be established. Only then, can true democracy, transparency, or shared governance, exist on campus. When students are part of the process, it is the most powerful lesson and learning experience any higher education institution can provide them.

SAM—YOU WILL RUE THE DAY

"The real voyage in discovery consists not in seeking new landscapes, but in having new eyes." This favorite quote from Marcel Proust struck Leslie as Founders University began the second month of classes in the spring semester. The last few months had been a whirlwind of activity on the campus as a new energy began to take hold. This new energy brought a dizzying array of excitement and a torqueing of the system. Some people were fired up and others were worried. Sam felt both, every day.

The folks at HEMetrics had spent several days, spread out over three visits, with different groups on campus. The purpose of these visits were "listening sessions." Several large group sessions were held along with several smaller focus groups. This was the topic of discussion at today's president's cabinet meeting. President Davis was briefed first thing in the morning by Dr. Xiong.

The conversation ran smoothly as Dr. Xiong shared with the cabinet the process used to solicit feedback from the various constituent groups and then the primary themes that emerged from across these bodies. Nothing stood out as unexpected or unusual. There were plenty of head nods affirming the findings. Meng then laid forth the structured process for fleshing out and developing the plan over the next several months. All went well until Sam broached what she thought was an innocent topic.

"I've been impressed," Sam began, with the breadth of coverage of our consultants. Indeed, they have spent a great deal of time with our folks. Nobody can say they didn't have a chance to be heard. Now that we will begin the more formalized structure of the strategic planning process, I think we need to make sure that these different groups have a formal 'seat at the table.'"

Lloyd scanned the room looking for body language feedback from his colleagues. He called on Peter Gabrielse. "Peter, it looks like you're itchin' to say something."

Peter hesitated. "Well, it's . . . ." He paused another moment. "It's just. . . . I don't know. The people have had their say. You said that yourself, Sam. Now, it's up to us around this table to carry out the mandate. Today's planning needs to be nimble. It can't get bogged down in academic debate and political correctness." These words started slowly, but they came rushing out at the end.

Henry Hutchins caught people a bit off guard as he played more of a peacekeeper mode. "I hear you, Peter. I've had some of the same thoughts. Maybe, though, it's more a matter of their role of involvement that needs to be considered."

Henry continued, "Sam taught me something earlier this year."

Sam didn't know what to think. She turned her head slightly to one side but kept keen eye contact with Henry. As he elaborated, she understood and smiled.

"When Sam pushed to reinvigorate the Faculty Senate committees, I have to admit I was both skeptical and anxious, quite frankly," Henry went on. "I felt rather conflicted when I met with the Senate's Budget Committee. I was afraid they wanted great detail to our budget, including salaries, and the like. But, that wasn't the case. They were simply thrilled to see our revenue streams, how much we relied on student tuition, and general operational and capital expenses. They were also interested, yet confused, by our endowment structure."

"But, Henry, "Peter continued, "Aren't you afraid of being on a slippery slope. You've opened up the floodgates, and now they'll want more . . . "

Henry interrupted. "No, I don't think so. We meet at the end of October, and they haven't asked for anything else from me. They were polite, asked good and fair questions, and thanked me."

Sam felt a bit emboldened. "In fact, I have heard discussions at the Senate meetings that are encouraging. They are thinking about how they can help with enrollments. Even more importantly, they started talking about student retention. They see that they share in this responsibility."

Lloyd Davis had a wry smile on his lips. Sam couldn't tell what he was thinking, but she continued. "As a matter of fact, the Senate is asking if Peter and Henry can come to their next meeting to talk about our endowment."

That remark landed with a thud. The wry smile remained on Lloyd's face, but it was not shared by his vice presidents. The conversation continued for another quarter of an hour with an expectant ebb and flow. President Davis concluded the meeting by announcing he was strongly considering requiring each academic program to offer an online/hybrid version of their programs. This would give students a choice between traditional face-to-face instruction and remote instruction. Sam was to lead the task force and plan for implementation within two years. At the end, the cabinet members left and hurried on to the tasks at hand for the day.

Within the hour, President Davis cast a shadow in Sam's office door. As he gently knocked on her door, he asked, "Sam, do you have a few minutes for me?"

Sam looked up from her computer. "Lloyd, please come in." She motioned for them to both sit at the small round table at the other side of her office. "What can I do for you?"

"I have quietly been watching you and your resolve to enhance shared governance on this campus. There's no doubt there is a new sense of excitement, but this two-sided coin also brings with it some concerns. I think it's getting to the point I need to insert myself a bit more."

"I'm sorry if this has been causing you concern, Lloyd," Sam quietly answered. "How can I help? How do you want to get more involved?"

"Those are kind of loaded questions, Sam," Lloyd went on. "I don't know if you have a master plan, so to speak, with empowering these groups. Or, are you just want to empower people and let it happen on its own? I'm rather ambivalent about either approach, honestly."

Sam wasn't sure how to respond, but she replied, "I don't have a master plan. I guess I have encouraged this to happen rather organically."

"I think that concerns me, Sam. We're the senior administration and we need to be in control. We're in charge; this is not a democracy. The Board of Trustees entrust us to carry out their vision, the University's mission."

Sam could tell Lloyd wasn't upset. He simply was speaking freely about his thoughts and his concerns. So she felt comfortable to add, "I don't think it's for us to 'control' the process." As soon as she uttered these words she wished she could take them back.

But, Lloyd was confident enough in himself that he didn't take offense. "You might be right, Sam. But, you might be wrong. So, I want to be more involved. I'd like to attend the next Staff Council meeting and the next SGA meeting. Could you please ask them for me to be placed on their next agendas?"

With all that said, Sam felt rather uncomfortable as President Davis left her office. She felt what she was doing was the right thing. So, why was it so hard?

Sam was serving as the administrative liaison to both the SGA and to the staff council. Her schedule made it impossible to attend all the meetings of either group. She felt badly about this, but there truly was nothing she could do. For example, she had not been able to attend the last two meetings of the SGA and only made one of the last four. It was in this context that she called Tiffany Jones—the SGA staff sponsor. Tiffany was also an associate dean of students.

Tiffany was delighted to receive Sam's call asking for President Davis to attend the next meeting. She updated Sam: "We've been doing a great deal of work since you last visited with us, Dr. Sabbon. Our SGA leadership team has been holding a number of focus groups with students."

Sam was caught off guard. She inquired, "What groups? What has been the focus?"

"Oh, you've got the students fired up. We have had focus groups of students living in the residence halls, veterans, nontraditional students, commuters, LGBT, and others. We're getting great feedback."

"I had no idea, Tiffany," came Sam's hesitating response. "What have you been asking them, and what is the feedback you've been receiving?"

Tiffany eagerly shared. "The senators are asking their fellow students how they want to be more involved in the governance of the campus and what kinds of concerns they have. But, don't worry, Dr. Sabbon. They also want to know their ideas for how to improve things and what their roles should be."

Sam was starting to get the feeling she was no longer in control. Was this all getting away from her? Maybe the cabinet members were right with their concern. Tiffany interrupted Sam's thinking.

"And, the SGA wants to present to you an award at this next meeting. It's supposed to be a surprise, but I want to make sure you're there. I'll keep the rest a secret, but I'm glad you can attend. The students are going to be so excited to see you!"

A couple of days had passed, and this time it was Sam's turn to visit President Davis's office. As she entered, she updated her chief executive. "Good morning, Lloyd. I have dates for you to put on your calendar for the next SGA and Staff Council meetings."

After they discussed the dates, Lloyd gave Sam his own update. "Sam, I have continued thinking about our last discussion on shared governance. You had talked about having the different constituent groups be given a seat at the table."

Sam's mind raced back to the last cabinet meeting. "Ah, yes, Lloyd. What are your thoughts?"

"As part of shared governance, faculty absolutely have a right for a seat at the table. In fact, I would go so far as to say they have a responsibility for a seat at the table. So, with that said, I'm going to have the Faculty Senate Chair or designee attend all of the Cabinet meetings for the time being. They may not always stay for the entire meeting, but they need to be a part of the dialogue." His voice trailed off at the end.

"I think that's a great idea, Lloyd," came Sam's response. "But, I think I might have heard some hesitancy in your voice."

"No, no, not really. I'm committed to the faculty voice at the table. It's the other groups."

Both Lloyd and Sam sat quietly for a moment, staring at one another. Sam felt the awkwardness, so she interjected. "What is your hesitancy, Lloyd?"

"I don't think I want the Staff Council at the table, and certainly not the Student Government. What I mean by that, Sam, is I don't think it's appropriate for them to serve on the Cabinet and attend those meetings."

"Oh, I see, Lloyd," Sam continued. "But, I never envisioned them attend our meetings."

Without pause, Lloyd went on. "However, their voices and their share of the responsibility is essential to the success of our strategic planning. Therefore, I want good representation from both the Staff Council and from the Student Government on all of our Strategic Planning initiative committees, as well as our Strategic Planning Steering Committee."

"Lloyd, that's brilliant. It's fantastic!" Sam extolled.

"I am asking you, Sam, to work with the other vice presidents, and with the Staff Council and SGA to find suitable representatives for all these committees. Let's jump on this and have them in place by the end of the month."

Sam left Lloyd's office with a new sense of purpose and excitement. As always, these feelings were accompanied by the panic of having a lot more work to do and the uncertainty of how to get it all done.

This Friday afternoon, the staff council was holding its monthly meeting. Lloyd Davis and Samantha Sabbon were both in attendance. Beatriz started the session by calling the meeting to order followed by approval of the minutes. She then turned her attention to a special announcement.

Beatriz stood up and positioned herself standing immediately behind Sam. "I am so thrilled to make a special presentation, today. By unanimous consent, our Staff Council is recognizing Dr. Samantha Sabbon with this month's Employee of the Month Award!"

After the applause subsided, Beatriz continued to a red-faced Sam. "Sam, you have meant the world to us. You have treated us with dignity and respected. You helped us to see ourselves as valued professionals who play a critical role every day at Founders University. We appreciate you!"

Sam didn't know what to say about the truly unexpected proclamation; she wiped away a tear. "You, my friends, mean everything to me. Your work and commitment to Founders is omnipresent." The group laughed as Sam continued. "Your stake in shared governance is important, not only because it's the right thing to do, but also because it's the right way to treat our colleagues. I thank you."

Beatriz next turned her attention to Lloyd Davis. "Dr. Davis, we're excited to have you join us, today. I turn the floor over to you, sir."

With that, President Davis spent the next twenty minutes reminding the staff of the strategic planning efforts to date and make plans to continue to move forward. He indicated that Sam would be working with them to request staff representation on all planning committees—both standing and ad hoc committees. He noted, "We need staff who have not only interest in certain initiatives, but also the ones who have special expertise in these same initiatives."

Camille raised her hand. After Dr. Davis nodded to her, she exclaimed, "This is so wonderful to hear, President Davis. As a matter of fact, we have been discussing an issue that is of interest to us, and some of us have expertise in."

"Great, Camille. What is it?" came Lloyd's reply.

"Many of us have concerns about a rumor we heard. We heard that we're going to move to online teaching. We're not one of those online universities. We're special because of our traditional, personal, and face-to-face teaching. That's who we are. Online is not a part of our vision or mission."

This exchange took both Sam and Lloyd by surprise. Lloyd finally responded. "Well, Camille, while I appreciate your thoughts, there's more to consider. It is the Board of Trustees' responsibility to set the vision of the university and to guard our mission—to make sure we are beholden to that mission. They hire me, and I hire you, to carry out their expectations."

Sam didn't know what to do. She sat there quietly and nodded in subtle agreement.

Lloyd concluded, "Dr. Sabbon and I will continue our conversation and keep you posted. We'll invite you to work with our committees as appropriate." With that, he thanked everyone and left the room.

The rest of the meeting was a blur to Sam. She couldn't even remember what was said over the next hour. Her mind kept racing back to the last half hour. As she left the meeting, President Davis was waiting for her outside.

"Oh, Dr. Davis, have I kept you waiting?" asked Sam.

Lloyd put his hand on Sam's shoulder. He had kind eyes and gave her a paternal smile. "Sam, please take my discussions with you seriously. I've admired what you're trying to do with democratic decision making. But, I need you to do it the right way."

"Of course, Lloyd," came Sam's feeble reply.

"I need you to be more active in keeping me posted. And, you and I need to start planning how we can be purposeful and systematic in empowering our community. We need to plan our expectations, processes and timelines, and provide training. In fact, I think our board will need this, too."

Sam nodded in agreement and began to feel a little better.

"Sam, start pulling some notes together. Let's the two of us get together next Thursday for lunch in my office. Please block off two hours. This is going to be critical and must happen concurrently with our other planning efforts."

Sam was thinking this was quite a way to end a busy week. But, she thanked Lloyd for his patience and direction.

Lloyd concluded their chat. "One other concern, Sam. I heard that some of the faculty senators want to be involved in putting together next year's budget. Find out what that's all about. We need to be transparent, but they aren't responsible for the budget—Henry is. Please work with him, too. Now, I have to have dinner with a possible donor to our university. I have to make her realistic about some of her far-out expectations."

As Sam turned to walk to her car after a long Friday afternoon, her cell phone buzzed. It was a text message.

> We shall not cease from exploration; And the end of all our exploring; Will be to arrive where we started; And know the place for the first time.[49]
>
> T. S. Eliot

NOTES

1. Jon Meacham, *The Soul of America: The Battle for our Better Angels* (New York: Random House, 2018), 44.

2. Larry Gerber, *The Rise and Decline of Faculty Governance: Professionalization and the Modern American University* (Baltimore, MD: Johns Hopkins University Press, 2014), 165.

3. Steven Bahls, "How to Make Shared Governance Work: Some Best Practices," *Trusteeship,* Association of Governing Boards (March/April 2014), 2. Gerber went on with a very prescient analysis on the topic and quoting Peter Drucker:

> Faculty must make the case to the American public that current trends, including the deprofessionalization of the faculty and the retreat from the practices of shared governance, pose a danger to the future well-being of American society. Even as the market model and a top-down approach to management have gained predominance in most aspects of American life, some voices outside academe have long recognized that in a "knowledge-based society" management ignores professional expertise at its peril. Management guru Peter Drucker thus argued as early as 1980 that the increasing importance of expertise and professional groups in modern "postindustrial" society would require "new, and fairly radical, organizational concepts." He predicted that the "hospital or the university will be a better model than the traditional military" as organizations become "concentric, overlapping, coordinated rings, rather than pyramids." Drucker concluded that there needed to be a recognition "that within given fields the professionals should set the standards and determine what their contribution should be." Rather than being an obstacle to "progress" and greater "efficiencies," a "collegial" form of shared governance represents a model that, in many respects, has made possible the success of many cutting-edge high-tech firms and companies in other areas of the economy that are especially dependent on the expertise and creativity of their knowledge workers (2).

4. AGB, *Shared Governance: Changing with the Times* (Washington, DC: AGB, 2017), 6.

5. Bjorn Stensaker and Agnete Vabo, "Re-inventing Shared Governance: Implications for Organisational Culture and Institutional Leadership," *Higher Education Quarterly* 67 (3), (2013), 264. These authors looked forward with regard to the future of governance systems: "At least two crucial dimensions can be identified. The first dimension concerns ways decisions are taken. Here, one may distinguish between decision-making processes that emphasise formal rules and regulations . . . and decision-making that is more informal where collegial processes are more characterized by reaching agreement and consensus dominate." 263.

6. William Bowen and Eugene Tobin, *Locus of Authority: The Evolution of Faculty Roles in the Governance of Higher Education* (Princeton University Press, 2015), 191.

7. Brian Mitchell and Joseph King, *How to Run a College: A Practical Guide for Trustees, Faculty, Administrators, and Policymakers* (Baltimore, MD: Johns Hopkins University Press, 2018), 10.

8. AGB, "Shared Governance: Is OK Good Enough?" (Washington, DC: AGB, 2016), 23.

9. Clark Kerr, "Governance and Functions," *Daedalus* 99 (1) (Winter 1970), 120.

10. Adrianna Kezar and Elizabeth Holcombe, "Shared Leadership in Higher Education: Important Lessons from Research and Practice," *American Council on Education* 29 (2017), 5.

11. AGB, *Shared Governance,* 6.

12. Stensaker and Vabo, "Re-inventing Shared Governance," 263.

13. Jean Lipman-Blumen, *The Connective Edge: Leading in an Interdependent World* (San Francisco: Jossey-Bass, 1996), 210.

14. Fritjof Capra, *The Hidden Connections: A Science for Sustainable Living* (New York: Anchor Books, 2004), 121. Much greater depth describing these new and natural organizational systems can be found in: Perry Rettig, *Quantum Leaps in School Leadership* (Lanham, MD: Rowman & Littlefied, 2002).

15. Bowen and Tobin, *Locus of Authority*, 210–211.

16. Roger Baldwin, "Navigating Board-Faculty Collaboration," *Trusteeship* (Washington, DC: AGB, 2018), 4.

17. Kezar and Holcombe, "Shared Leadership in Higher Education," 2. Citing the work of Margaret Wheatley. They add: "[S]hared leadership ultimately improves the implementation of organizational decisions since members dedicate time and energy up front to fostering a shared vision and collective ownership in organizational actions." 13.

18. Stensaker and Vabo, "Re-inventing Shared Governance," 271.

19. Robert Scott, *How University Boards Work: A Guide for Trustees, Officers, and Leaders in Higher Education* (Baltimore, MD: Johns Hopkins University Press, 2018), 12.

20. Colleen Flaherty, "Survey of Presidents and Board Members Suggest Shared Governance Matters to them But Could be Improved Upon," *Inside Higher Ed.* (2016), 3.

21. Mitchell and King, *How to Run a College*, 17.

22. Robert Scott, *How University Boards Work*, 6.

23. AGB, *Shared Governance*. 9.

24. Scott, *How University Boards Work*, 98.

25. Terrence MacTaggart, *Leading Change: How Boards and Presidents Build Exceptional Academic Institutions* (Washington, DC: AGB Press 2011), 48.

26. Philip Altbach, "Harsh Realities: The Professoriate Faces a New Century," In Philip Altbach, Robert Berdahl, and Patricia Gumport, eds, *American Higher Education in the Twenty-First Century: Social, Political, and Economic Challenges* (Baltimore, MD: Johns Hopkins University Press, 2005), 29.

27. Clara Chan, "A Common Plea of Professors: Why Can't My Faculty Senate Pull More Weight?" *The Chronicle of Higher Education* (July 6, 2017), 1.

28. AGB, "Shared Governance," 11.

29. Bowen and Tobin, *Locus of Authority*, 173.

30. Ibid., 167.

31. Ibid., 208.

32. Gerber, *The Rise and Decline of Faculty Governance,* 166.

33. Patrick Dolan, *Restructuring Our Schools: A Primer on Systemic Change* (Kansas City: Systems & Organization, 1994), 65.

In addition, the reader is invited to review the formal academic staff bylaws of the University of Wisconsin Oshkosh (2008) at: www.uwosh.edu/sas/about-senate/academic-staff-bylaws/view. This document provides codified detail to the staff's formal structure and involvement in shared governance at the university and as part of the larger University of Wisconsin System. Specifically, Section GOV 4.1 in the UW Oshkosh Faculty and

Academic Staff Handbook states, in part: "The academic staff members . . . shall be active participants in the immediate governance of and policy development for the institution. The academic staff members have the primary responsibility for the formulation and review, and shall be represented in the development, of all policies and procedures concerning academic staff members, including academic staff personnel matters."

34. Scott, *How University Boards Work*, 62–63.

35. Ibid., 62.

36. Ibid., 4.

37. Bowen and Tobin, *Locus of Authority*, 138.

38. AGB, "Effective Governing Boards" 24.

39. Mitchell and King, *How to Run a College*, 17.

40. Scott, *How University Boards Work*, 67.

41. Bahls, "How to Make Shared Governance Work," 3–6.

42. AGB, "AGB Board of Directors' Statement on Shared Governance" (Washington, DC: AGB, 2017), 5–9.

43. Paulo Freire, *Pedagogy of the Oppressed* (New York: Continuum, 1970).

44. George Cheney et al., "Democracy, Participation, and Communication at Work: A Multidisciplinary Review," *Communication Yearbook* 21 (2004), 72–73.

45. Teresa Harrison, "Designing the Post-Bureaucratic Organization: New Perspectives on Organizational Change," *Australian Journal of Communication* 19 (1992), 24.

46. Viviane Robinson, "Critical Theory and the Social Psychology of Change," In Keith Leithwood et al. eds, *International Handbook of Educational Leadership and Administration* (1996), 1085–1086.

47. Elisabeth Backman and Bernard Trafford, *Democratic Governance of Schools* (Council of Europe Publishing, 2007), 78. These authors continue, "It may be [the democratic leader's] job to ensure that there is a balance of opinion within the group and that good practice is observed; in other words, that minorities are represented." 82.

48. AGB, "Effective Governing Boards," 2014.

49. T. S. Eliot, *Four Quartets* (New York: Harcourt, 1943).

Bibliography

Altbach, Philip. "Harsh Realities: The Professoriate Faces a New Century." In *American Higher Education in the Twenty-First Century: Social, Political, and Economic Challenges*, edited by Philip Altbach, Robert Berdahl, and Patricia Gumport. Baltimore, MD: Johns Hopkins University Press, 2005.

Altbach, Philip. "Patterns in Higher Education Development." In *American Higher Education in the Twenty-First Century: Social, Political, and Economic Challenges,* edited by Philip Altbach, Robert Berdahl, and Patricia Gumport. Baltimore, MD: Johns Hopkins University Press, 2005.

Altbach, Philip, Robert Berdahl, and Patricia Gumport, eds. *American Higher Education in the Twenty-First Century: Social, Political, and Economic Challenges.* Baltimore, MD: Johns Hopkins University Press, 2005.

American Association of University Professors. "Protecting Academic Freedom." Washington, DC: American Association of Professors, 2017a, www.aaup.org/our-work/protecting-academic-freedom.

American Association of University Professors. "Shared Governance." Washington, DC: American Association of University Professors, 2017b, www.aaup.org/our-programs/shared-governance.

American Association of University Professors. "Statement on Government of Colleges and Universities." Washington, DC: American Association of University Professors, 1966. www.aaup.org/report/statement-government-colleges-and-universities.

American Association of University Professors. "Statement on Government of Colleges and Universities." Washington, DC: American Association of University Professors, 2017c, www.aaup.org/report/statement-government-colleges-and-universities.

Association of Governing Boards of Universities and Colleges. "AGB Board of Directors' Statement on Shared Governance." Washington, DC: AGB, 2017a.

Association of Governing Boards of Universities and Colleges. "Effective Governing Boards: A Guide for Members of Governing Boards of Independent Colleges and Universities." Washington, DC: AGB, 2014.

Association of Governing Boards of Universities and Colleges. "Shared Governance: Changing with the Times." Washington, DC: Association of Governing Boards and College, 2017b.

Association of Governing Boards of Universities and Colleges. "Shared Governance: Is OK Good Enough?" Washington, DC: Association of Governing Boards and Colleges, 2016.

Atkinson, Anthony. "The Promise of Employee Involvement." *CMA Magazine* 3 (April 1990): 8.

Bachrach, Peter, and Aryeh Botwinick. *Power and Empowerment: A Radical Theory of Participatory Democracy.* Philadelphia: Temple University Press, 1992.

Backman, Elisabeth, and Bernard Trafford. *Democratic Governance of Schools.* Council of Europe Publishing, 2007.

Bahls, Steven. "Evolving Workforce Expectations." In *Trusteeship.* Association of Governing Boards of Universities and Colleges, Summer 2018.

Bahls, Steven. "How to Make Shared Governance Work: Some Best Practices." In *Trusteeship.* Association of Governing Boards, March/April 2014.

Bahls, Steven. *Shared Governance in Times of Change: A Practical Guide for Universities and Colleges.* Association of Governing Boards, 2014.

Baldwin, Roger. "Navigating Board-Faculty Collaboration." In *Trusteeship.* Association of Governing Boards of Universities and Colleges, Summer 2018.

Beyer, L. "The Value of Critical Perspectives in Teacher Education." *Journal of Teacher Education* 2 (March/April 2001): 52.

Birnbaum, Robert, and Peter Eckel. "The Dilemma of Presidential Leadership." In *American Higher Education in the Twenty-First Century: Social, Political, and Economic Challenges.* Baltimore, MD: Johns Hopkins University Press, 2005.

Blau, Peter. *The Organization of Academic Work.* New York: Wiley, 1973.

Block, Peter. *Stewardship: Choosing Service Over Self-Interest.* San Francisco: Berrett-Koehler, 1996.

Bowen, William, and Eugene Tobin. *Locus of Authority: The Evolution of Faculty Roles in the Governance of Higher Education.* Princeton, NJ: Princeton University Press, 2015.

Capra, Fritjof. *The Hidden Connections: A Science of Sustainable Living.* New York: Anchor Books, 2004.

Carpenter-Hubin, Julie, and Lydia Snover. "Key Leadership Positions and Performance Expectations." In *Organization and Administration in Higher Education,* edited by Kristina Powers and Patrick Schloss. New York, NY: Routledge, 2017.

Chan, Clara. "A Common Plea of Professors: Why Can't My Faculty Senate Pull More Weight?" *The Chronicle of Higher Education* (July 6, 2017).

Cheney, G., et al. "Democracy, Participation, and Communication at Work: A Multidisciplinary Review." *Communication Yearbook* 21, 2004.

Chomsky, Noam. *Chomsky: On Miseducation.* Lanham, MD: Rowman & Littlefield, 2000.

CIVITAS: *A Frame Work for Civic Education,* A Collaborative Project of the Center for Civic Education and the Council for the Advancement of Citizenship, National Council for the Social Studies Bulletin, No. 86, 1991.

Clarke, John H. "Growing High School Reform: Planting the Seeds of Systemic Change." *NASSP Bulletin* (April 1999): 4, 8, and 9.

Clarke, John. *Personalized Learning.* Lanham, MD: Rowman & Littlefield Education, 2002.

Cleaver, Eldridge. *Soul on Ice.* New York: Dell Publishing, 1968.

Csikszentmihalyi, Mihalyi. *Flow: The Psychology of Optimal Experience.* New York: Harper Collins, 1990.

Davis, E., and Russell Lansbury, eds. *Democracy and Control in the Workplace.* Melbourne, Australia: Longman and Cheshire, 1986.

DeWitt, S. *Worker Participation and the Crisis of Liberal Democracy.* Boulder, CO: Westview Press, 1980.

Diamond, Larry. https://web.standford.edu/~ldiamond/iraq/DemocracyEducation0 204.htm (as of Spring 2019).

Dolan, Patrick. *Restructuring Our Schools: A Primer on Systemic Change.* Kansas City: Systems & Organization, 1994.

Donnellon, Anne, and Maureen Scully. "Teams, Performance, and Rewards: Will the Post-Bureaucratic Organization be a Post-Meritocratic Organization?" In *The Post-Bureaucratic Organization: New Perspectives on Organizational Change,* edited by Charles Heckscher and Lynda Applegate. Thousand Oaks, CA: Sage, 1994.

Dotlich, D. and P. Cairo. *Unnatural Leadership: Going Against Intuition and Experience to Develop Ten New Leaderships Instincts.* San Francisco: Jossey-Bass, 2002.

Eliot, T. S. *Four Quartets.* New York: Harcourt, 1943.

Flaherty, Colleen. "Survey of Presidents and Board Members Suggests Shared Governance Matters to them but could be Improved Upon." *Inside Higher Ed.,* 2016. https://www.insidehighered.com/news/2016/09/29/survey-presidents-and-board-members-suggests-shared-governance-matters-them-could-be?width=775&hei ght=500&iframe=true.

Freire, Paulo. *Pedagogy of the Oppressed.* New York: Continuum, 1970.

Fung, Archon. *Empowering Participation: Reinventing Urban Democracy.* Princeton, NJ: Princeton University Press, 2004.

Fung, Archon and Erik Wright eds. *Deepening Democracy: Institutional Innovations in Empowered Participatory Governance.* London, England: Verso, 2003.

Gamson, Zelda, and Henry Levin. "Obstacles to the Survival of Democratic Organizations." In *Worker Cooperatives in America,* edited by Robert Jackal and Henry M. Levin. Berkeley, CA: University of California Press, 1984, 223.

Gerber, Larry. "College and University Governance: How the AAUP has Established Widely Accepted Norms of Shared Governance." In *American Association of University Professors.* Washington, DC, January–February, 2015, www.aaup.org/article/college-and-university-governance.

Gerber, Larry. *The Rise and Decline of Faculty Governance: Professionalization and the Modern American University.* Baltimore, MD: Johns Hopkins University Press, 2014.

Green, Reginald. *Practicing the Art of Leadership: A Problem-Based Approach to Implementing the ISLLC Standards.* Upper Saddle River, NJ: Merrill Prentice Hall, 2001.

Greenberg, Edward. *Workplace Democracy: The Political Effects of Participation.* Ithaca, NY: Cornell University Press, 1986.

Gumport, Patricia, and Stuart Snydman. "The Formal Organization of Knowledge: An Analysis of Academic Structure." *The Journal of Higher Education* 73 (2002): 383.

Halal, William. *The New Management: Bringing Democracy and Markets Inside Organizations.* San Francisco: Berrett-Koehler, 1998.

Harrison, Teresa. "Designing the Post-Bureaucratic Organization: Toward Egalitarian Organizational Structure." *Australian Journal of Communication* 19 (2) (1992): 14–29.

Heckscher, Charles. "Defining the Post-Bureaucratic Type." In *The Post-Bureaucratic Organization: New Perspectives on Organizational Change,* edited by Charles Heckscher and Anne Donnellon. Thousand Oaks, CA: Sage, 1994.

Heckscher, Charles and Anne Donnellon, eds. *The Post-Bureaucratic Organization: New Perspectives on Organizational Change.* Thousand Oaks, CA: Sage, 1994.

Heifetz, Ron. *Leadership Without Easy Answers.* Cambridge, MA: Harvard University Press, 1994, 121, http://usconstitution.net/consttop_cnb.html.

Huntington, Samuel. *The Clash of Civilizations: Remaking of World Order.* New York: Simon & Schuster, 1997, 71.

Jermier, J. "Critical Perspectives on Organizational Control." *Administrative Science Quarterly* (1998): 43.

Kerr, Clark. "Governance and Functions." *Daedalus* 99 (1) (Winter 1970): 108–121, www.jstor.org/stable/20023936.

Kezar, Adrianna and Elizabeth Holcombe. "Shared Leadership in Higher Education: Important Lessons from Research and Practice." Washington, DC: American Council on Education, 2017.

Lachs, John. "Shared Governance is a Myth." *The Chronicle of Higher Education* (February 6, 2011).

Leithwood, Kenneth, et al. eds. *International Handbook of Educational Leadership and Administration.* Amsterdam: Kluwer Academic Publishers, 1996.

Lipman-Blumen, Jean. *The Connective Edge: Leading in an Interdependent World.* San Francisco: Jossey-Bass, 1996.

Lounder, Andy. *Shared Governance: Is OK Good Enough?* Washington, DC: Association of Governing Boards of Universities and Colleges, 2016.

MacTaggart, Terrence. *Leading Change: How Boards and Presidents Build Exceptional Academic Institutions.* Washington, DC: AGB Press, 2011.

MacTaggart, Terrence. "Nontraditional Presidents: A New Wave of Enterprise Leadership." In *Trusteeship.* Association of Governing Boards of Universities and Colleges, Summer 2018.

March, James, and Johan Olsen. *Democratic Governance.* New York: The Free Press, 1995.

Marion, Russ. *Leadership in Education: Organizational Theory for the Practitioner.* Upper Saddle River, NJ: Merrill Prentice Hall, 2002.

McGregor, Douglas. *The Human Side of Enterprise.* New York: McGraw-Hill, 1960.

Meacham, Jon. *The Soul of America: The Battle for Our Better Angels.* New York: Random House, 2018.

Melear, Kerry. "The Role of Internal Governance, Committees, and Advisory Groups." In *Organization and Administration of Higher Education,* edited by Kristina Powers and Patrick Schloss. New York, NY: Routledge, 2017.

Minzberg, Henry. *The Structuring of Organizations.* Englewood Cliffs, NJ: Prentice-Hall, 1979.

Mitchell, Brian and Joseph King. *How to Run a College: A Practical Guide for Trustees, Faculty, Administrators, and Policymakers.* Baltimore, MD: Johns Hopkins University Press, 2018.

Neumann, Francis., Jr. "Organizational Structures to Match the New Information-Rich Environments: Lessons from the Study of Chaos." *Public Productivity and Management Review* 21 (September 1997).

Niebuhr, Reinhold. *Reinhold Niebuhr: Major Works on Religion and Politics,* edited by Elisabeth Sifton. New York Library of America, 1944.

Nohria, Nitin and James D. Berkley. "The Virtual Organization: Bureaucracy, Technology, and the Implosion of Control." In *The Post-Bureaucratic O4ganization: New Perspectives on Organizational Change,* edited by Charles Heckscher and Lynda Applegate. Thousand Oaks, CA: Sage, 1994.

Olson, Gary. "Exactly What is 'Shared Governance'?" *The Chronicle of Higher Education* (July 23, 2009).

O'Neil, Robert. "Academic Freedom: Past, Present, and Future beyond September 11." In *American Higher Education in the Twenty-First Century: Social, Political, and Economic Challenges,* edited by Philip Altbach and Patricia Gumport. Baltimore, MD: Johns Hopkins University Press, 2005.

Orwell, George. *1984.* London, England: Secker and Warburg, 1949.

Owens, Robert. *Organizational Behavior in Education: Adaptive Leadership and School Reform.* New York: Pearson Allyn & Bacon, 2004.

Powers, Kristina and Patrick Schloss, eds. *Organization and Administration in Higher Education,* 2nd ed. New York, NY: Routledge, 2017.

Ramsay, Harvie. "Industrial Democracy and the Question of Control." In *Democracy and Control in the Workplace,* edited by E. Davis and Russell Lansbury. Melbourne, Australia: Longman and Cheshire, 1986.

Responsibility Centered Management, www.indiana.edu/~obap/rcm-iub.php.

Rettig, Perry. *Quantum Leaps in School Leadership.* Lanham, MD: Rowman & Littlefield, 2002.

Rettig. Perry. *Reframing Decision Making in Education: Democratic Empowerment of Teachers and Parents.* Lanham, MD: Rowman & Littlefield, 2016.

Rhodes, L. "Connecting Leadership and Learning." *A Planning Paper Developed for the American Association of School Administrators National Center for Connected Learning* (April 1997).

Robinson, Viviane. "Critical Theory and the Social Psychology of Change." In *International Handbook of Educational Leadership and Administration,* edited by Kenneth Leithwood, et al. Amsterdam: Kluwer Academic Publishers, 1996.

RUSH. "Closer to the Heart." *A Farewell to Kings.* Mercury Records, 1977.

Schmidtlein, Frank and Robert Berdahl. "Autonomy and Accountability: Who Controls Academe?" In *American Higher Education in the Twenty-First Century: Social, Political, and Economic Challenges,* edited by Philip Altbach and Patricia Gumport. Baltimore, MD: Johns Hopkins University Press, 2005.

Scott, Robert. *How University Boards Work: A Guide for Trustees, Officers, and Leaders in Higher Education.* Baltimore, MD: Johns Hopkins University Press, 2018.

Seltzer, Rick. "New Books Examine College Governance and How it can Adapt to Changing Times." *Inside Higher Ed* (March 1, 2018).

Sergiovanni, Thomas and Robert Starratt. *Supervision: A Redefinition.* New York: McGraw-Hill, 1993.

Smyth, John. "The Socially Just Alternative to the 'Self-Managing School.'" In *International Handbook of Educational Leadership and Administration,* edited by Keith Leithwood et al. The Netherlands: Kluwer Academic Publishers, 1996.

Stensaker, Bjorn and Agnete Vabo. "Re-inventing Shared Governance: Implications for Organisational Culture and Institutional Leadership." *Higher Education Quarterly* 67 (3) (July 2013): 256–274.

Tzu, Sun. *The Art of War.* Translated in English by Samuel B. Griffith. 5th Century B.C. Oxford: Oxford University Press, 1963.

Voronov, Maxim and Peter T. Coleman. "Beyond the Ivory Towers: Organizational Power Practices and a 'Practical' Critical Post-modernism." *The Journal of Applied Behavioral Science* 39 (2) (June 2003).

University of Wisconsin Oshkosh. *Academic Staff Bylaws,* 2008, www.uwosh.edu/s as/about-senate/academic-staff-bylaws/view.

Wainwright, Hilary. *Reclaim the State: Experiments in Popular Democracy.* London: Verso, 2003.

Washington & Jefferson. College Decision Matrix. *American Council on Education,* 2017, www.acenet.edu/news-room/Documents/Washington-and-Jefferson-Colle ge-Decision-Matrix.pdf.

Weisbuch, Robert. "Down with Downsizing the Liberal Arts. A Survival Guide for Small College." *Chronicle of Higher Education* (October 2016): 14.

Wells, Richard, and J. Stevens Picou. "The Becoming Place: A Study of Educational Change in a Small College." *Research in Higher Education* 1 (1982): 17.

Whealler-Johnston, Susan. "Sharing Governance." In *Trusteeship.* Association of Governing Boards of Universities and Colleges, Summer 2018.

Whealler-Johnston, Susan. "Why Boards Should Care About Shared Governance." In *Trusteeship.* Association of Governing Boards of Universities and Colleges, September/October 2017.

Wheatley, Margaret. *Leadership and the New Science: Learning about Organizations from an Orderly Universe.* San Francisco: Berrett-Koehler, 1994.

Wilson, Woodrow. *Constitutional Government in the United States,* 36. New York: Columbia University Press (cited in John Meacham, 2018).

www.constitutioncenter.org/explore/TheUS.Constitution/index.shmtl.

www.loc.gov/law/help/guide/federal/usconst.php.

www.uwosh.edu/sas/about-senate/academic-staff-bylaws/view.

Zakaria, Fareed. *The Future of Freedom: Illiberal Democracy at Home and Abroad.* New York: W. W. Norton & Company, 2003.

Zinn, Howard. *Declarations of Independence: Cross-Examining American Ideology.* New York: Harper Collins, 1990.

Zusman, Ami. "Challenges Facing Higher Education in the Twenty-First Century." In *American Higher Education in the Twenty-First Century: Social, Political, and Economic Challenges,* edited by Philip Altbach and Patricia Gumport. Baltimore, MD: Johns Hopkins University Press, 2005.

About the Author

Dr. Rettig has been an educator for thirty-six years with a breadth of leadership experiences. He has written extensively on the topic of leadership and has presented his thoughts to dozens of audiences across the globe. *Shared Governance* is his fifth book with Rowman & Littlefield, and it challenges the weakening governance model of contemporary American higher education. He does this be reexamining the original model of shared governance with an overlay of the nation's founding principles and then reimagines what a newer model might look like.

After a dozen years as a teacher and as a school administrator in K–12 public schools, Rettig became a professor of educational administration and leadership. The past twenty-five years have found him in higher education serving in various capacities as a faculty member, associate vice chancellor, vice president for academic affairs, and most recently as vice president for enrollment management. He has served as a leadership fellow and as interim deans in the school of education and the school of nursing and health sciences. Presently, Dr. Rettig serves as the vice president for enrollment management and vice president for the Athens Campus at Piedmont College in Georgia where he continues to maintain his faculty credentials.

Made in United States
North Haven, CT
13 March 2022

17069230R00090